Background Knowledge for Academic Subjects

Fundamental Reading

Michael A. Putlack
Stephen Poirier
Tony Covello

PLUS 1

DARAKWON

Fundamental Reading PLUS ①

Publisher Chung Kyudo
Authors Michael A. Putlack, Stephen Poirier, Tony Covello
Editors Jeong Yeonsoon, Zong Ziin, Kim Namyeon
Designers Park Narae, Elim

First published in January 2020
By Darakwon, Inc.
Darakwon Bldg., 211, Munbal-ro, Paju-si, Gyeonggi-do 10881
Republic of Korea
Tel: 82-2-736-2031 (Ext. 250)
Fax: 82-2-732-2037

ISBN 978-89-277-0859-9 54740
978-89-277-0856-8 54740 (set)

www.darakwon.co.kr

Photo Credits
Kimm Otto (p. 24), MarcoPachiega (p. 26), Ververidis Vasilis (p. 27), Simon Pittet
(p. 41), goga18128 (p. 61), Plateresca (p. 61), travelview (p. 80), Jonathan Weiss
(p. 82), Fecundap stock (p.82), Sheila Fitzgerald (p. 82), Sarah Marchant (p. 95),
davidsansegundo (p. 97) / www.shutterstock.com
Gleilson Miranda / Governo do Acre (p. 19), File:Índios isolados no Acre 12.jpg
betsyprioleau.com (p.40), File:William Segar Sir Walter Raleigh 1598.jpg
Pedro Szekely (p.40), File:Gold Museum, Bogota (36145671394).jpg
John Tenniel (p.54), File:Punch Anti-Irish propaganda (1882) Irish Frankenstein.jpg
(p. 54) File:From the Earth to the Moon Jules Verne.jpg
April Nobile (p. 68), Ficheiro: Gracilidris pombero casent0010797 profile 1.jpg
(p. 68), File:Laonastes aenigmamus - young male JP Hugot PLOS ONE.jpg /
https://commons.wikimedia.org/wiki/
(p. 54) https://www.flickr.com/photos/paul_garland/3949891395/in/photostream/

Components Main Book / Workbook
12 11 10 9 8 7 6   24 25 26 27 28

Fundamental Reading

PLUS 1

DARAKWON

How to Use This Book

This book has 8 chapters that cover different academic subjects. Each chapter is composed of 2 units based on interesting topics related to the subject.

Student Book

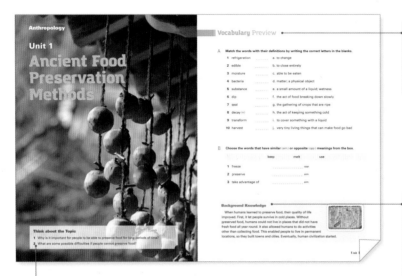

Vocabulary Preview

Students can learn the key words from the passage and get ready to read.

Background Knowledge

Students can read brief information that will help them predict and understand the main reading passage.

Think about the Topic

Two warm-up questions are provided to motivate students to think about the topic before continuing with the unit.

QR code for listening to the passage

Main Reading Passage

The passages discuss topics that have been carefully chosen to provide academic knowledge as well as to interest students. Each passage is between 260–290 words long.

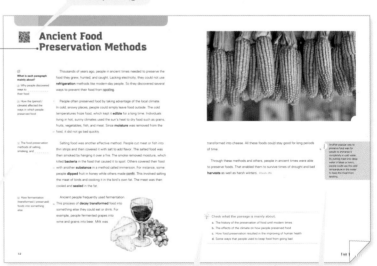

Finding the topic of each paragraph

Finding the main topic or main idea of the passage

Additional information and further learning about the topic

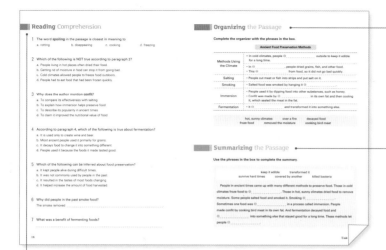

Organizing the Passage

By completing a graphic organizer or a Fill in a Table question, students can review and recognize important ideas and information presented in the passage.

Summarizing the Passage

By completing a regular summary or a Prose Summary question, students can review the main points of the passage once again.

Reading Comprehension

5 multiple-choice questions and 2 short-answer questions are given to help students master various types of questions.

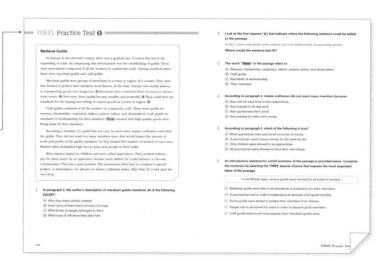

TOEFL Practice Test

At the end of the book, there is a supplementary TOEFL Practice Test section containing four passages. Each passage has five or six questions similar to ones that frequently appear on real TOEFL tests.

Workbook

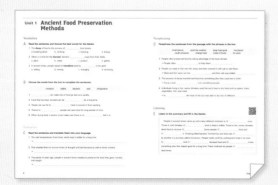

The first part contains 4 types of exercises, which provide students with a deeper understanding of the passage as well as enhanced vocabulary and language skills.

The second part presents a writing topic related to the reading passage. Students can develop their thoughts on the topic, conduct further research on their own, and learn to write a short paragraph.

Table of Contents

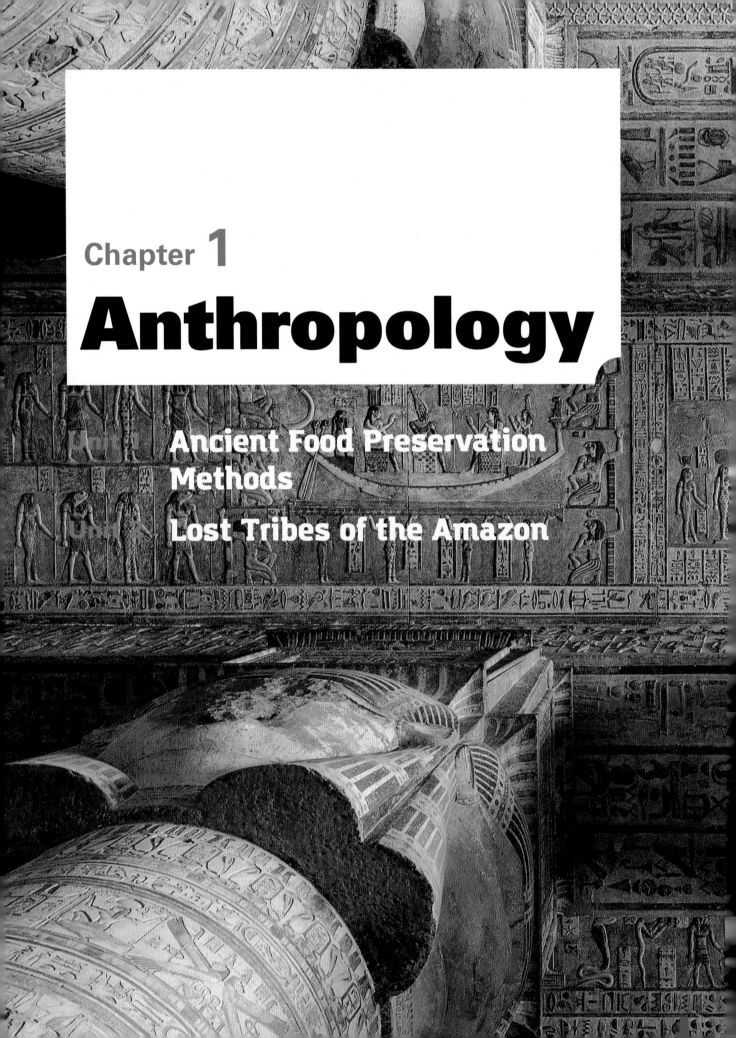

Chapter **1**

Anthropology

Ancient Food Preservation
Methods

Lost Tribes of the Amazon

Anthropology is the scientific study of humans and how they behaved in the past. Anthropologists study human cultures, especially ancient ones, and learn how they developed over time.

Unit 1
Ancient Food Preservation Methods

Think about the Topic

1 Why is it important for people to be able to preserve food for long periods of time?

2 What are some possible difficulties if people cannot preserve food?

Vocabulary Preview

A **Match the words with their definitions by writing the correct letters in the blanks.**

1 refrigeration _____ a. to change

2 edible _____ b. to close entirely

3 moisture _____ c. able to be eaten

4 bacteria _____ d. matter; a physical object

5 substance _____ e. a small amount of a liquid; wetness

6 dip _____ f. the act of food breaking down slowly

7 seal _____ g. the gathering of crops that are ripe

8 decay (n.) _____ h. the act of keeping something cold

9 transform _____ i. to cover something with a liquid

10 harvest _____ j. very tiny living things that can make food go bad

B **Choose the words that have similar (sim.) or opposite (opp.) meanings from the box.**

	keep	melt	use

1 freeze _____ opp.

2 preserve _____ sim.

3 take advantage of _____ sim.

Background Knowledge

When humans learned to preserve food, their quality of life improved. First, it let people survive in cold places. Without preserved food, humans could not live in places that did not have fresh food all year round. It also allowed humans to do activities other than collecting food. This enabled people to live in permanent locations, so they built towns and cities. Eventually, human civilization started.

Ancient Food Preservation Methods

Q

What is each paragraph mainly about?

P1 Why people discovered ways to _____ their food

P2 How the (period / climate) affected the ways in which people preserved food

P3 The food preservation methods of salting, smoking, and _____

P4 How fermentation (transformed / preserved) foods into something else

Thousands of years ago, people in ancient times needed to preserve the food they grew, hunted, and caught. Lacking electricity, they could not use **refrigeration** methods like modern-day people. So they discovered several ways to prevent their food from spoiling.

5 People often preserved food by taking advantage of the local climate. In cold, snowy places, people could simply leave food outside. The cold temperatures froze food, which kept it **edible** for a long time. Individuals living in hot, sunny climates used the sun's heat to dry food such as grains, fruits, vegetables, fish, and meat. Since **moisture** was removed from the
10 food, it did not go bad quickly.

Salting food was another effective method. People cut meat or fish into thin strips and then covered it with salt to add flavor. The salted food was then smoked by hanging it over a fire. The smoke removed moisture, which killed **bacteria** in the food that caused it to spoil. Others covered their food
15 with another **substance** in a method called immersion. For instance, some people **dipped** fruit in honey while others made confit. This involved salting the meat of birds and cooking it in the bird's own fat. The meat was then cooled and **sealed** in the fat.

Ancient people frequently used fermentation.
20 This process of **decay transformed** food into something else they could eat or drink. For example, people fermented grapes into wine and grains into beer. Milk was

transformed into cheese. All these foods could stay good for long periods of time.

Through these methods and others, people in ancient times were able to preserve foods. That enabled them to survive times of drought and bad **harvests** as well as harsh winters. Words 283

25

i Another popular way to preserve food was for people to immerse it completely in cold water. By putting meat into deep water in lakes or rivers, people could use the cold temperature in the water to keep the meat from spoiling.

 Check what the passage is mainly about.

a. The history of the preservation of food until modern times

b. The effects of the climate on how people preserved food

c. How food preservation resulted in the improving of human health

d. Some ways that people used to keep food from going bad

Reading Comprehension

1 The word spoiling in the passage is closest in meaning to

    a. rotting   b. disappearing   c. cooking   d. freezing

2 Which of the following is NOT true according to paragraph 2?

    a. People living in hot places often dried their food.

    b. Getting rid of moisture in food can stop it from going bad.

    c. Cold climates allowed people to freeze food outdoors.

    d. People had to eat food that had been frozen quickly.

3 Why does the author mention confit?

    a. To compare its effectiveness with salting

    b. To explain how immersion helps preserve food

    c. To describe its popularity in ancient times

    d. To claim it improved the nutritional value of food

4 According to paragraph 4, which of the following is true about fermentation?

    a. It is used only to create wine and beer.

    b. Most ancient people used it primarily for grains.

    c. It decays food to change it into something different.

    d. People used it because the foods it made tasted good.

5 Which of the following can be inferred about food preservation?

    a. It kept people alive during difficult times.

    b. It was not commonly used by people in the past.

    c. It resulted in the tastes of most foods changing.

    d. It helped increase the amount of food harvested.

6 Why did people in the past smoke food?

    The smoke removed _____ .

7 What was a benefit of fermenting foods?

    _____

Organizing the Passage

Complete the organizer with the phrases in the box.

Ancient Food Preservation Methods

Methods Using the Climate	• In cold climates, people ❶_____ outside to keep it edible for a long time.
	• In ❷_____, people dried grains, fish, and other food. • This ❸_____ from food, so it did not go bad quickly.
Salting	• People cut meat or fish into strips and put salt on it.
Smoking	• Salted food was smoked by hanging it ❹_____.
Immersion	• People used it by dipping food into other substances, such as honey. • Confit was made by ❺_____ in its own fat and then cooling it, which sealed the meat in the fat.
Fermentation	• It ❻_____ and transformed it into something else.

> hot, sunny climates   over a fire   decayed food
> froze food   removed the moisture   cooking bird meat

Summarizing the Passage

Use the phrases in the box to complete the summary.

> keep it edible   transformed it
> survive hard times   covered by another   killed bacteria

People in ancient times came up with many different methods to preserve food. Those in cold climates froze food to ❶_____. Those in hot, sunny climates dried food to remove moisture. Some people salted food and smoked it. Smoking ❷_____. Sometimes one food was ❸_____ in a process called immersion. People made confit by cooking bird meat in its own fat. And fermentation decayed food and ❹_____ into something else that stayed good for a long time. These methods let people ❺_____.

Unit 2

Lost Tribes of the Amazon

Think about the Topic

1 What do you think an uncontacted tribe is?

2 Where do you believe uncontacted tribes may live?

Vocabulary Preview

A **Match the words with their definitions by writing the correct letters in the blanks.**

1 immense _____ a. simple; basic

2 tribe _____ b. very large

3 uncontacted _____ c. a rule made by the government

4 ancestor _____ d. not having spoken or met with others

5 primitive _____ e. a person whose job is to cut down trees

6 hut _____ f. a weapon with a sharp point on a long stick

7 spear _____ g. a small home made of materials like wood or grass

8 logger _____ h. a member of a person's family who lived previously

9 trafficker _____ i. a group of people who live together and are often related

10 law _____ j. a person who buys or sells something illegal, such as drugs

B **Choose the words that have similar** (sim.) **or opposite** (opp.) **meanings from the box.**

official	straight	tiny

1 immense _____ opp.

2 formal _____ sim.

3 directly _____ sim.

Background Knowledge

The Amazon Rainforest is the largest tropical rainforest in the world. It covers parts of nine countries in South America. There are at least 40,000 species of plants in the Amazon. There are also thousands of species of birds, fish, mammals, and reptiles. More than 2.5 million insect species are there. There are more than 400 tribes living in the rainforest, too. About fifty of them have not had contact with modern-day people.

Lost Tribes
of the Amazon

The Amazon Rainforest covers an **immense** area of land in nine countries in South America. Among them are Brazil, Peru, Colombia, and Venezuela. The forest is deep, dark, and dangerous. Nevertheless, groups of people have lived there for thousands of years. These are the lost **tribes** of the
5 Amazon.

Q

What is each paragraph mainly about?

P2 _____ people and how they live their lives

Members of lost tribes are also called **uncontacted** people. This is not exactly true though because most tribes are aware of the outside world. There are only a few that have never made contact with modern people. These lost tribes follow the ways of their **ancestors**, so they lead **primitive**
10 lives. They survive by hunting and fishing. They farm and gather fruits, nuts, and plants as well.

P3 The _____, weapons, and educations of lost tribes

The homes of lost tribes are simple **huts** made of wood and straw. In addition, the tribe members' clothes are made of natural materials. As for weapons, they hunt with **spears**, darts, and bows and arrows. Finally, there
15 is no system of formal education. Children learn directly from their parents and older members of their communities. Their educations focus on how to survive in the jungle.

P4 (How / Where) lost tribes have been harmed in recent years

In recent years, members of lost tribes have suffered at the hands of
20 modern-day people. ❶ **Loggers**, gold miners, and drug **traffickers** have been moving into their lands. ❷ These individuals sometimes kill tribespeople by shooting them. ❸ In
25 other cases, they spread diseases to tribe members. ❹

▲ A gold mining place

18

▲ The huts of lost tribes

Fortunately, the governments of many South American countries are attempting to protect these lost tribes. **Laws** have been passed to keep them safe. People are forbidden from entering large sections of the forest, too. This allows the tribes to live in peace away from the modern world. **Words 289**

How governments are (harming / helping) lost tribes

 Check the main idea of the passage.

a. The Amazon Rainforest is full of many different lost tribes.

b. Uncontacted people lead lives very different from other people.

c. It is important to introduce members of lost tribes to modern society.

d. More laws must be passed to take care of uncontacted people.

i One major problem that uncontacted tribes suffer from is logging. Loggers cut down huge forested areas, which reduces the land that uncontacted tribes can live on. Thus many have to move even deeper into the jungle.

Reading Comprehension

1 In paragraph 2, why does the author mention uncontacted people?

   a. To describe where most of them live

   b. To compare them with modern people

   c. To explain why a term is not accurate

   d. To argue that they can adapt to modern life

2 In paragraph 3, all of the following questions are answered EXCEPT:

   a. Who teaches the children of tribe members?

   b. What do tribe members use to hunt with?

   c. What do the schools of uncontacted tribes look like?

   d. What materials are used to make tribe members' homes?

3 Where would the following sentence best fit in paragraph 4?

> Their lack of resistance to these illnesses has resulted in some tribes getting completely wiped out.

   a. ❶   b. ❷   c. ❸   d. ❹

4 The word forbidden in the passage is closest in meaning to

   a. rejected   b. attacked   c. banned   d. proposed

5 Which of the following is NOT true about the lost tribes of the Amazon Rainforest?

   a. They are protected by laws passed by different countries.

   b. Some of them were killed by people from the outside world.

   c. They have lived in the Amazon Rainforest for a long period of time.

   d. Some of them have lifestyles like those of people in the modern world.

6 What do the educations of the tribes focus on?

Their educations _____.

7 Who has been moving into the lands of lost tribes?

_____

Organizing the Passage

Complete the organizer with the phrases in the box.

Lost Tribes of the Amazon

Who Uncontacted People Are	• They are members of lost tribes, but many have had contact with ❶_____.
How They Live	• They live like their ancestors did, so their lives are primitive. • They live in simple huts made of ❷_____. • They hunt with spears, darts, and bows and arrows. • They have ❸_____ but focus on how to survive in the jungle.
How They Have Been Harmed	• Loggers, gold miners, and drug traffickers have been moving into their lands. • Some of these people shoot tribe members or ❹_____.
How Governments Are Helping	• They have ❺_____ to protect lost tribes. • They are forbidding people from ❻_____ of the rainforest.

give them diseases	entering large sections	wood and straw
no formal education	the outside world	passed laws

Summarizing the Passage

Use the phrases in the box to complete the summary.

	in the jungle	natural materials	
live primitive lives		banning people	kill tribe members

There are uncontacted tribes living deep in the Amazon Rainforest in South America. Most of them have had contact with the outside world, but they still ❶_____. They live in huts and wear clothes made of ❷_____. They hunt for food. Their educations focus on surviving ❸_____. Loggers, gold miners, and drug traffickers have been moving into their lands. They sometimes ❹_____ or give them diseases. Governments have passed laws to help them and are ❺_____ from entering parts of the rainforest. These let tribe members live in peace.

Chapter 2
Psychology

Psychology is the scientific study of the mind and behavior. Psychologists study the minds of people and try to determine why individuals and groups act in certain manners. They also focus on people's and groups' characteristics and the reasons that they have those characteristics.

Unit 3
Mob Mentality

Think about the Topic

1 Do you like to follow your friends' behavior when you are with them?

2 Why do people suddenly change their personalities when they are in large groups?

Vocabulary Preview

A **Match the words with their definitions by writing the correct letters in the blanks.**

1 preference _____ a. unable to be seen

2 mentality _____ b. a way of thinking

3 herd _____ c. full of passion or interest

4 riot (v.) _____ d. to become involved in; to take part in

5 interaction _____ e. the act of holding back or controlling oneself

6 engage in _____ f. a large group of animals, such as cows or deer

7 enthusiastic _____ g. something that is currently popular or in style

8 trend _____ h. to behave badly and often violently in public

9 invisible _____ i. something that one likes more than another thing

10 restraint _____ j. the act of being with or doing activities with others

B **Choose the words that have similar** (*sim.*) **or opposite** (*opp.*) **meanings from the box.**

passionate	group	peaceful

1 crowd _____ *sim.*

2 violent _____ *opp.*

3 enthusiastic _____ *sim.*

Background Knowledge

The actions of crowds often have negative results.
However, in some cases, they can result in positive actions.
For instance, when there is an accident or injury, people in a
crowd are more likely to help others than an individual person
would. In addition, crowds have started revolutions that have
resulted in social changes.

Mob Mentality

Q

What is each paragraph mainly about?

P1 (What / Where) mob mentality is

People often make decisions based on personal **preferences** or by how they can benefit. But at times, people give up their own desires and follow those of a larger group. In psychology, this pattern of behavior is known as mob **mentality**.

P2 Some _____ created when people think of herd mentality

5 Two other names for this behavior are crowd mentality and **herd** mentality. These terms often create images of crowds of people **rioting** in the streets in 10 most people's minds. Riots are an example of herd mentality. But

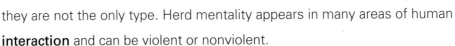

they are not the only type. Herd mentality appears in many areas of human **interaction** and can be violent or nonviolent.

P3 Some common _____ of _____ violent herd mentality

Street riots are the most common examples of violent herd mentality. 15 These may result from people **engaging in** protests. They might initially gather for peaceful purposes. Then, something, such as police actions, causes _____. Other street riots happen when fans celebrate a sports victory. The fans get overly **enthusiastic** and violent. They burn cars and damage buildings.

P4 A (violent / nonviolent) example of herd mentality

20 A nonviolent example of herd mentality is when people follow **trends**. Black Friday is one trend. It is the day after Thanksgiving in the United States. Stores have big sales on this day, so they attract people. Others see people shopping, so they decide to go shopping, too. On this day, shoppers often seem to lose their minds by trying to buy as much as they 25 can. This is an example of nonviolent herd mentality.

▲ Crowds on Black Friday © Ververidis Vasilis

People engage in herd mentality for various reasons. They might feel safe following others. Some believe that if something is good for one person, then it is good for them, too. Others feel **invisible** in crowds, so they lose all feelings of **restraint**. They engage in activities that they would not normally do and simply follow the crowd. Words 291

P5 (When / Why) people may engage in herd mentality

i Mob mentality is very common in economics. When people see trends in markets, large numbers may act the same way. This can cause stock markets rapidly to go up or down considerable amounts. The result is often negative for many investors.

 Check what the passage is mainly about.

a. The dangers of people acting the same when in groups

b. Some examples of how people may behave in groups

c. The differences between mob mentality and herd mentality

d. Results of what happens when people engage in mob mentality

Reading Comprehension

1 Which of the following is true according to paragraph 2?
   a. Herd mentality is not always violent.
   b. Crowd mentality is different from herd mentality.
   c. Riots only happen when people act the same way.
   d. Mob mentality usually results in people getting hurt.

2 The word initially in the passage is closest in meaning to
   a. obviously   b. sincerely   c. carefully   d. firstly

3 What is the best choice for the blank?
   a. a violent response
   b. a change in plans
   c. people to leave
   d. nothing serious

4 Why does the author mention Black Friday?
   a. To point out that it takes place after Thanksgiving each year
   b. To show how it is a nonviolent example of mob mentality
   c. To remark that it is a common trend in the United States
   d. To explain the importance of shopping in American culture

5 In paragraph 5, which is NOT mentioned as a reason people engage in herd mentality?
   a. They believe it is safe to act like others.
   b. They do not feel restrained while in a crowd.
   c. They think they can break the law if they are with others.
   d. They believe something good for others is good for them.

6 What does the underlined this pattern of behavior refer to?
   It refers to when people give up _____.

7 What seems to happen to shoppers on Black Friday?

   _____

Organizing the Passage

Complete the organizer with the phrases in the box.

	Mob Mentality
What It Is	• It happens when people give up ❶ _____ and follow those of a larger group. • It can be ❷ _____ .
Violent Examples	• It may happen when people ❸ _____ . • People celebrating a sports victory may become violent.
Nonviolent Example	• ❹ _____ in the United States is a nonviolent example. • People visit stores having big sales and seem to lose their minds by trying to buy as much as they can.
Why People Engage in It	• They ❺ _____ following others. • They think something good for others is good for them, too. • They lose restraint because they ❻ _____ in crowds.

violent or nonviolent	Black Friday	feel invisible
their own desires	feel safer	engage in protests

Summarizing the Passage

The first sentence of a short summary is provided below. Complete the summary by choosing THREE answer choices that express the most important ideas.

Mob mentality can be violent or nonviolent and happens for various reasons.

1 Mob mentality is also called crowd mentality and herd mentality.

2 People may feel safer following others and lose feelings of restraint that make them act like others.

3 On Black Friday in the United States, shoppers engage in the nonviolent activity of shopping at sales.

4 Most people do not wish to engage in mob mentality but simply follow what others are doing.

5 Large crowds may become violent when celebrating a sports victory or when protesting something.

Psychology

Unit 4

Amnesia

Think about the Topic

1 What can cause a person to suffer memory loss?

2 How difficult do you think it would be to live with memory loss?

Vocabulary Preview

A **Match the words with their definitions by writing the correct letters in the blanks.**

1 condition _____ a. extreme; harsh

2 permanent _____ b. a sickness or a medical issue

3 assume _____ c. happening before something else

4 adjust _____ d. to change and get used to a new situation

5 sufferer _____ e. to begin to have a particular quality

6 previous _____ f. to get back something that one once had

7 traumatic _____ g. continuing forever or for a very long time

8 severe _____ h. to take place for a certain amount of time

9 regain _____ i. extremely painful to one's mind or thoughts

10 last (v.) _____ j. a person who has a sickness or other problem

B **Choose the words that have similar** (*sim.*) **or opposite** (*opp.*) **meanings from the box.**

temporary	recover	latter

1 former _____ *opp.*

2 permanent _____ *opp.*

3 regain _____ *sim.*

Background Knowledge

It is possible for people to improve the health of their brain. This can help them improve their memory and stop them from forgetting things. For instance, some foods have nutrients such as omega-3 fatty acids, which improve brain functions. These include oily fish such as salmon and tuna. Other foods, including dark chocolate, blueberries, and almonds, contain different nutrients that can improve a person's memory.

Amnesia

Q

What is each paragraph mainly about?

P1 When amnesia happens and the ways in which it can (hurt / affect) people

P2 What the (symptoms / types) of retrograde amnesia are

P3 What happens to people with _____ amnesia

P4 How _____ amnesia may last for people

Some people may suffer from memory loss at times. Known as amnesia, this **condition** tends to occur when people have head injuries or catch certain diseases. The type of memory loss varies. It can be either short term or **permanent**. It can also affect a large number of memories or just 5 one or two.

Amnesia can **assume** many forms. Two types of it are the most common though. They are *retrograde and *anterograde amnesia. A person who is unable to remember events before a certain date has the former. The date is usually when the person suffered brain damage. This person is capable 10 of forming new memories. But the individual is unable to recall events from the past.

Anterograde amnesia is the opposite of retrograde amnesia. A person can recall past events but cannot form any new memories. A person with this type of amnesia often has difficulty **adjusting** 15 to life. After all, **sufferers** forget what happens each day after their injuries. Thus they cannot remember any new friends they make. Nor can they recall the activities they did the **previous** day.

20 In some cases, the effects of amnesia are permanent. This may happen to a person when a **traumatic** event such as a violent attack or a car 25 accident takes place.

Remember

The event is very **severe**, so the sufferer has no memory of it. Yet most people with amnesia **regain** their memories in a short time. It may only **last** a few hours or days. For others, it could take months or years to remember. Still, over time, most people remember what they once could not. Words 267

*retrograde: moving backward
*anterograde: moving forward

i There is no medicine that people with amnesia can take to improve their condition. Mostly, therapists try to get sufferers to use their existing memories to create new ones or to recover ones that they lost.

 Check the main idea of the passage.

a. The effects of amnesia can often cause difficulties for sufferers.

b. Doctors are still trying to figure out ways to help people with amnesia.

c. People with any type of amnesia may lose their memories permanently or temporarily.

d. Amnesia causes large numbers of people around the world to lose their memories.

Reading Comprehension

1 In paragraph 1, which of the following is mentioned about amnesia?

   a. How doctors usually try to treat it

   b. What often makes people get it

   c. What makes people recover from it

   d. How many people suffer from it

2 The word recall in the passage is closest in meaning to

   a. revise   b. report   c. remember   d. return

3 The word they in the passage refers to

   a. any new memories

   b. sufferers

   c. their injuries

   d. any new friends

4 According to paragraph 3, which of the following is NOT true about anterograde amnesia?

   a. Its opposite form is retrograde amnesia.

   b. People with it have trouble later in life.

   c. It makes people unable to form new memories.

   d. Diseases affecting the brain are the primary cause of it.

5 In paragraph 4, all of the following questions are answered EXCEPT:

   a. What types of memories may people forget temporarily?

   b. How long does amnesia last for many people with it?

   c. Does amnesia tend to be permanent or temporary for most people?

   d. What might cause a person to have a permanent case of amnesia?

6 When does amnesia tend to occur?

   It tends to occur when _____ .

7 What happens to a person with retrograde amnesia?

_____

Organizing the Passage

Complete the organizer with the phrases in the box.

Amnesia	
What It Is	• It is a condition that causes people to ❶ _____ . • Head injuries or ❷ _____ often cause it.
Retrograde Amnesia	• This happens when a person cannot ❸ _____ before a certain date. • It is often caused by brain damage.
Anterograde Amnesia	• This happens when a person can remember the past but cannot ❹ _____ . • People with this type of amnesia often have difficulty adjusting to life.
How Long It Lasts	• It may be permanent when people endure traumatic events such as ❺ _____ or car accidents. • Most people ❻ _____ in a few hours or days.

regain their memories	violent attacks	remember events
form new memories	certain diseases	lose their memories

Summarizing the Passage

Use the phrases in the box to complete the summary.

	a certain date	permanent amnesia
a head injury	adjusting to life	anterograde amnesia

People may suffer from memory loss after getting ❶ _____ or a disease. People with amnesia usually get one of two main types. Retrograde amnesia occurs when a person cannot remember events before ❷ _____ . However, people with it can form new memories. People with ❸ _____ can remember the past but cannot form new memories. These individuals usually have difficulty ❹ _____ . Amnesia can be permanent or temporary. Most sufferers recover quickly. But those experiencing traumatic events such as car accidents or violent attacks may get ❺ _____ .

Chapter 3
History

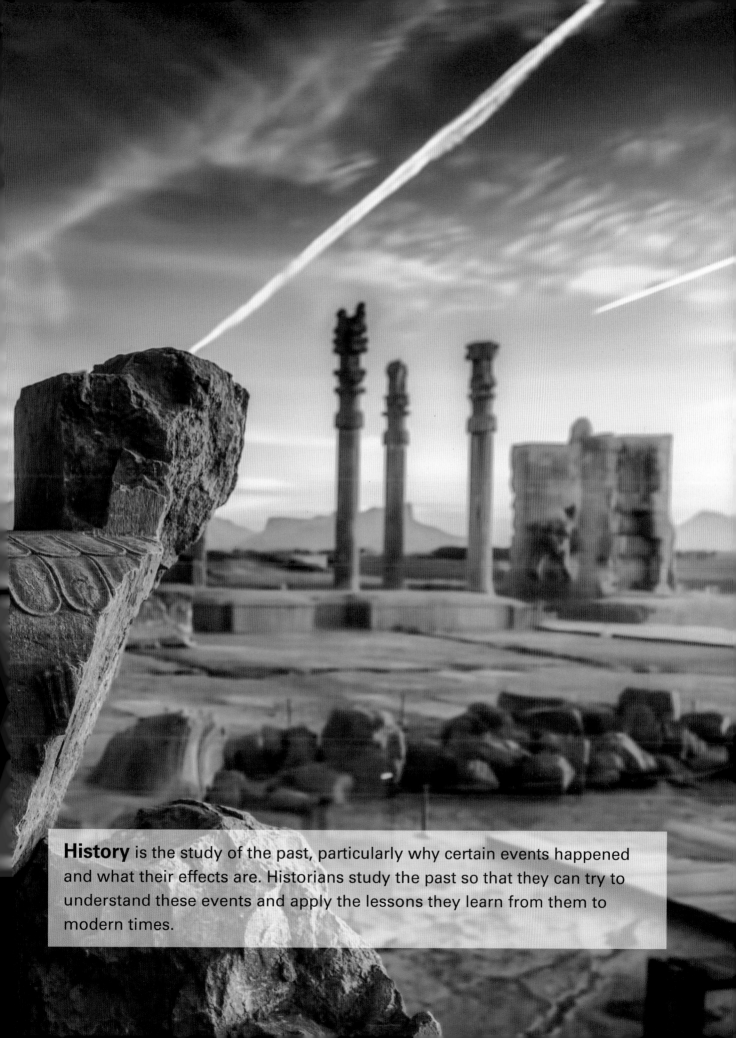

History is the study of the past, particularly why certain events happened and what their effects are. Historians study the past so that they can try to understand these events and apply the lessons they learn from them to modern times.

Unit 5
The Search for El Dorado

Think about the Topic

1 What are some lost worlds and lost cities that you know about?

2 Why are people so fascinated by lost worlds and lost cities?

Vocabulary Preview

A **Match the words with their definitions by writing the correct letters in the blanks.**

1 expedition _____   a. to kill

2 explorer _____   b. to defeat in battle

3 supposedly _____   c. the leader of a tribe

4 entirely _____   d. completely; totally

5 myth _____   e. assumed to be true

6 chief _____   f. a trip of discovery

7 conquer _____   g. the act of dying from a lack of food

8 convince _____   h. to make a person believe something is true

9 execute _____   i. a person who travels to discover new things

10 starvation _____   j. a story from the past that people believe but which is not true

B **Choose the words that have similar (*sim.*) or opposite (*opp.*) meanings from the box.**

partly	fight	acquire

1 obtain _____ *sim.*

2 battle _____ *sim.*

3 entirely _____ *opp.*

Background Knowledge

After Christopher Columbus discovered the New World—North and South America—in 1492, many Europeans sailed there. They wanted to explore the land and obtain treasure from it. They often fought tribes for their gold, silver, and jewels and were interested in learning where rich places were.

The Search for El Dorado

Q

What is each paragraph mainly about?

P1 Why the _____ and others searched for El Dorado

P2 How the (truth / myth) of El Dorado came to be

In the 1500s and 1600s, the Spanish sent numerous **expeditions** to South America. One goal was to obtain gold and silver. The Spanish and other **explorers** heard stories about a place called El Dorado. **Supposedly** a city made **entirely** of gold, it was searched for by many explorers.

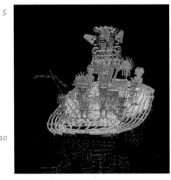

▲ The Muisca raft

5 Unfortunately for them, _____. The **myth** of El Dorado arose due to a custom by the Muisca people of Colombia. Whenever a new **chief** rose to power, there was a special ceremony. His body was covered in 10 gold dust, and he dived into a lake. The water washed the gold off while members of the tribe threw gold and gems into the lake. The Spanish called the chief *el dorado*, meaning "one covered in gold." Later, the story changed. Instead of a man covered in gold, there was a city made 15 of gold called El Dorado.

P3 What happened to Sir Walter Raleigh on his _____

The Spanish **conquered** the Muisca in 1538. They found plenty of gold but no El Dorado. Yet the story **convinced** many explorers, greedy for gold, to travel to the 20 New World. English explorer Sir Walter Raleigh was one of them. He led two expeditions in search of El Dorado. Both failed, and his son died in a battle with the Spanish. Raleigh was then **executed** after 25 returning to England for starting a war with the Spanish.

▲ Sir Walter Raleigh

▲ The lake of Guatavita where the myth of El Dorado originates

Later expeditions searched far and wide across South America. None was successful. In addition, explorers and their men were often killed by disease, **starvation**, and natives. The age of El Dorado expeditions finally ended in the late 1600s. Some people today still believe it exists though. They claim it is hidden by the jungle and is waiting for some brave explorers to find it. Words 287

🄿 The (results / success) of the search for El Dorado

30

Check the main point of the passage.

a. El Dorado was a city made of gold.

b. Nobody was ever able to find El Dorado.

c. The Spanish wanted gold in South America.

d. Sir Walter Raleigh was a great explorer.

i One benefit of the search for El Dorado was that explorers mapped large areas of South America. Many went deep into the Amazon Rainforest, and some of them even sailed on parts of the Amazon River.

Reading Comprehension

1 What is the best choice for the blank?

    a. the city never existed

    b. they did not believe the stories

    c. they did not know about El Dorado

    d. they found gold and silver elsewhere

2 The word arose in the passage is closest in meaning to

    a. appeared   b. told   c. remembered   d. approached

3 In paragraph 2, all of the following questions are answered EXCEPT:

    a. What did the Spanish call the chief?

    b. Why did the Muisca people cover their chief with gold dust?

    c. How was the story that the Spanish heard changed from the truth?

    d. Why did the Muisca people cover their buildings with gold?

4 Why does the author mention English explorer Sir Walter Raleigh?

    a. To discuss the war that he started in detail

    b. To blame him for getting his son killed

    c. To describe the results of his search for El Dorado

    d. To compare his actions with those of the Spanish

5 In paragraph 4, which of the following can be inferred about El Dorado?

    a. Many stories have been written about it.

    b. It definitely existed sometime in the past.

    c. Some of the expeditions looking for it succeeded.

    d. Some people will likely look for it in the future.

6 Why did explorers and their men die?

They were often _____.

7 What happened after the chief of the Muisca dived into the lake?

_____

Organizing the Passage

Complete the organizer with the phrases in the box.

The Search for El Dorado

Expeditions in South America	• The Spanish tried to find ❶_____ in South America in the 1500s and 1600s. • They also heard about a city made entirely of gold called El Dorado.
The Myth of El Dorado	• The Muisca people of Colombia had ❷_____ for a new chief. • They covered their chief in gold dust and had him jump into a lake. • They called the chief *el dorado*, meaning "❸_____," but the story changed to a city made of gold.
The Results of the Search for El Dorado	• The Spanish were unable to ❹_____. • Explorers such as Sir Walter Raleigh also failed to find the city. • ❺_____ failed, and men on them were killed by disease, starvation, and natives. • Some people think El Dorado exists and is ❻_____

a special ceremony	all other expeditions	find El Dorado
hidden by the jungle	gold and silver	one covered in gold

Summarizing the Passage

The first sentence of a short summary is provided below. Complete the summary by choosing THREE answer choices that express the most important ideas.

Many explorers looked for the city of El Dorado, but it did not actually exist.

1 The Muisca people used to put gold dust on their bodies when a new chief rose to power.

2 Explorers such as Sir Walter Raleigh tried to find El Dorado, but they failed.

3 The Spanish were the first to search for El Dorado once they heard about a city made of gold.

4 Some people believe that El Dorado is still hidden somewhere deep in the jungle.

5 Large numbers of groups looked for El Dorado until the 1600s, but they often died for various reasons.

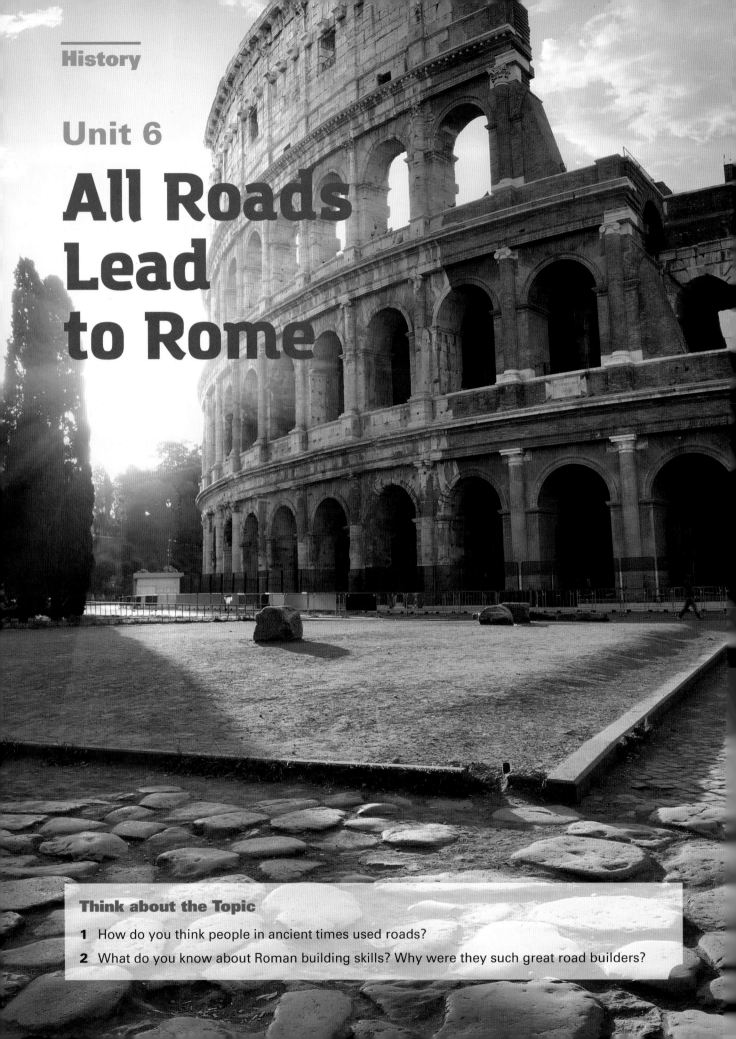

Unit 6
All Roads Lead to Rome

Think about the Topic

1 How do you think people in ancient times used roads?

2 What do you know about Roman building skills? Why were they such great road builders?

Vocabulary Preview

A **Match the words with their definitions by writing the correct letters in the blanks.**

1 idiom _____ a. widespread; broad

2 outstanding _____ b. excellent; very good

3 extensive _____ c. to have or own

4 possess _____ d. to change the path of something

5 obstacle _____ e. a long, deep, and narrow hole in the ground

6 drain _____ f. something that is blocking a person or thing

7 divert _____ g. a city where a country's or state's government is

8 trench _____ h. to remove the water or other liquid from something

9 decorative _____ i. having objects that make something look nicer or prettier

10 capital _____ j. an expression with a meaning different from that of the words in it

B **Choose the words that have similar** (*sim.*) **or opposite** (*opp.*) **meanings from the box.**

crooked	source	continue

1 last (*v.*) _____ *sim.*

2 straight _____ *opp.*

3 origin _____ *sim.*

Background Knowledge

Rome was the biggest and most important city in the Roman Empire. The Romans traveled frequently. For instance, its greatest families sent their children to other parts of the empire to rule, to serve in the military, and to run farms. The Romans also engaged in trade throughout the empire. For those reasons, the Romans made sure to build long-lasting roads.

All Roads Lead to Rome

Q

What is each paragraph mainly about?

P1 Where the _____ "All roads lead to Rome" originated

P2 How (well-made / extensive) the Roman road system was

P3 The way in which the Romans made _____ roads

P4 (Why / How) the Romans made long-lasting roads

"All roads lead to Rome" is a popular English **idiom** meaning that while there may be different ways to accomplish something, they all have the same result. The origins of this idiom go back centuries to the Roman Empire.

5 By the second century A.D., the Roman Empire occupied land from Spain in the west, to England in the north, to Turkey in the east, and to North 10 Africa in the south. People could travel to some parts of the empire by ship, but they mostly traveled on land. The

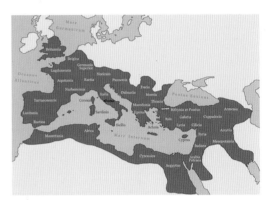

▲ The Roman Empire in 117 A.D. at its greatest extent

Romans, who were **outstanding** engineers, developed an **extensive** road 15 system. At one point, the empire **possessed** more than 400,000 kilometers of roads.

The Romans attempted to make their roads straight. For example, the ninety-kilometer road from Rome to Terracina was completely straight. The Romans preferred to avoid turns, so they built roads straight through natural 20 **obstacles**. They **drained** marshes, **diverted** creeks, cut forests, tunneled through mountains, and built bridges over rivers just to have straight roads.

They also built roads intended to last. First, they dug **trenches** and filled them with sand or dirt. Then, they added a layer of large stones set in cement. Next, they added a third layer 25 of smaller crushed rocks set in cement. The top layer was

▲ Basalt

a **decorative** one made of basalt, a volcanic rock. The roads were wide enough for both foot traffic and wheeled vehicles. In addition, they were so well made that some remain today.

Most importantly, the roads were built so that they eventually led to Rome. This allowed the Romans to travel from their **capital** to anywhere in the empire as directly as possible. And that is how the English idiom came to be. **Words 284**

30

i One of the first and most important Roman roads was the Appian Way. It was built in 312 B.C. and connected Rome to the southeastern part of Italy. It was used by the military and regular people for hundreds of years.

 Check what the passage is mainly about.

  a. The process the Romans used to make roads

  b. Why some Roman roads have survived until today

  c. The fastest method of travel in the Roman Empire

  d. How and why the Romans built many roads

Reading Comprehension

1   The word accomplish in the passage is closest in meaning to

   a. satisfy   b. consider   c. achieve   d. imagine

2   In paragraphs 2 and 3, which of the following CANNOT be inferred about the Romans?

   a. They created a huge empire.

   b. They were very good at building roads.

   c. They did not like making roads with turns.

   d. They could travel to every part of the empire by land.

3   Which of the following is true about Roman roads according to the passage?

   a. They were built in three layers.

   b. Crushed rocks were in their first layer.

   c. Only vehicles were able to use them.

   d. Some went over rivers and through mountains.

4   The word they in the passage refers to

   a. smaller crushed rocks

   b. the roads

   c. foot traffic

   d. wheeled vehicles

5   What does the underlined part in the passage mean?

   a. was created

   b. sounded

   c. stopped being used

   d. changed its meaning

6   What was the top layer of a Roman road made of?

   It was made of _____.

7   What does "All roads lead to Rome" mean?

   _____

Organizing the Passage

Complete the organizer with the phrases in the box.

All Roads Lead to Rome

The Roman Road System	• The Roman Empire occupied an enormous ❶_____. • The Romans had an ❷_____ that contained more than 400,000 kilometers of roads.
How the Romans Built Roads	• The Romans preferred to make ❸_____ and avoided turns. • They built straight roads through marshes, forests, and mountains and ❹_____.
How the Romans Made Long-lasting Roads	• They filled trenches with ❺_____ and then added large stones set in cement. • Next, they added smaller crushed rocks set in cement and then put basalt, a volcanic rock, on top. • The Romans made their roads so that they all eventually ❻_____.

led to Rome   amount of land   sand or dirt

extensive road system   straight roads   went over rivers

Summarizing the Passage

Use the phrases in the box to complete the summary.

exist today   went to Rome

large and small rocks   kilometers of roads   natural obstacles

The idiom "All roads lead to Rome" was based on the fact that all roads in the Roman Empire eventually ❶_____. The Romans had an extensive road system with more than 400,000 ❷_____. The Romans preferred straight roads, so they built their roads through ❸_____. They made roads with ❹_____, cement, and basalt. The roads were wide enough for foot traffic and wheeled vehicles. They were so well made that some of them ❺_____.

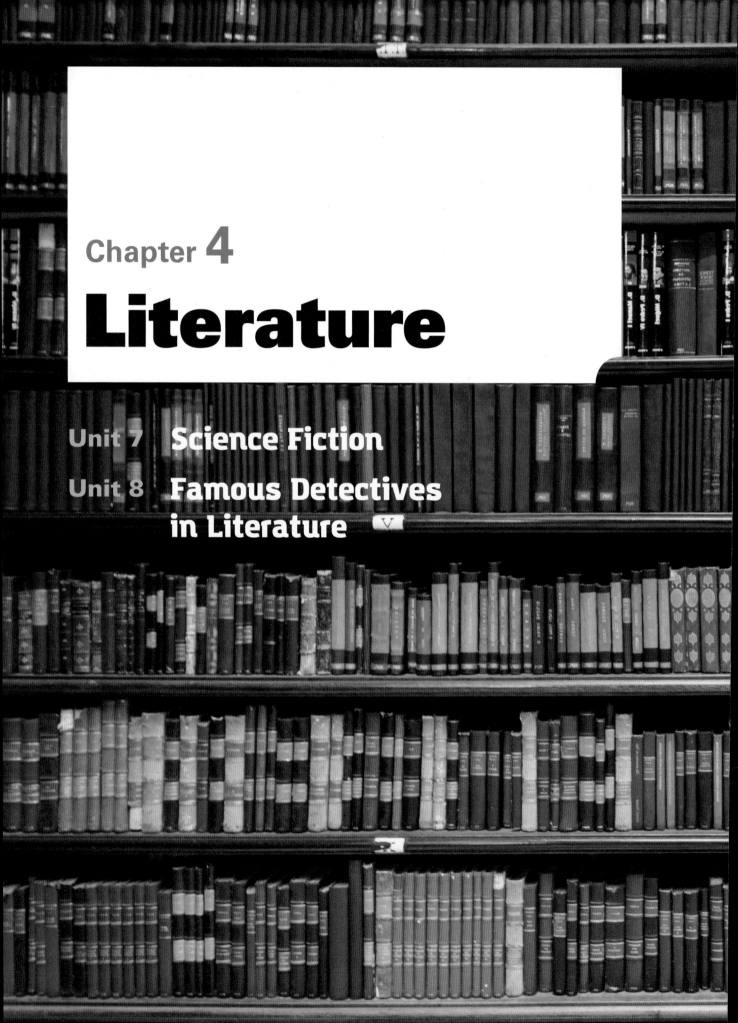

Chapter 4
Literature

Literature is any material that is written. This includes nonfiction works as well as works of fiction. Popular works of fiction include novels, stories, myths, legends, poems, and plays.

Unit 7
Science Fiction

Vocabulary Preview

A   **Match the words with their definitions by writing the correct letters in the blanks.**

1 publish _____   a. to create

2 genre _____   b. to move forward; to advance

3 speculative _____   c. a being from another planet

4 alien _____   d. relating to the act of ruling others

5 pose _____   e. an exciting or unusual experience

6 progress (v.) _____   f. relating to guesses or imagination

7 invasion _____   g. the act of entering another land as an enemy

8 adventure _____   h. to print something like a newspaper, magazine, or book

9 political _____   i. a person with special powers and who uses them for good

10 superhero _____   j. a particular type of artistic activity such as literature or art

B   **Choose the words that have similar** (sim.) **or opposite** (opp.) **meanings from the box.**

attack	native	emphasize

1 alien _____ opp.

2 stress (v.) _____ sim.

3 invasion _____ sim.

Background Knowledge

Some writing from centuries ago contained aspects of science fiction. But most people state that the genre began in the nineteenth century. Then, there were great advances made in many fields of science. Because science was so frequently in the news, writers began creating stories that used certain elements of it. This was how the genre of science fiction was created.

Science Fiction

Q

What is each paragraph mainly about?

P1 What science fiction is and _____ created it

P2 What early science-fiction authors _____ on

P3 How science-fiction (topics / authors) changed as the genre progressed

P4 Political and environmental topics in science-fiction works in the (nineteenth / twentieth) century

▲ *Frankenstein*

In 1818, Mary Shelley **published** *Frankenstein*, one of the greatest works in English literature. At the same time, she created the first real work of science fiction. This is a **genre** in literature that focuses on science. Often called "**speculative** fiction," lots of science-fiction stories are about science and technology, **aliens**, and other worlds.

10   The first few decades of science fiction focused on science and technology and the dangers they **posed**. For example, *Frankenstein* was about a man who attempts to create life. While he is successful, the monster he creates destroys not only that man but also the people he loves. *Strange Case of Dr. Jekyll and Mr. Hyde* by Robert Louis Stevenson
15 was another work about a mad scientist.

As science-fiction writing **progressed**, it began looking to the stars. Jules Verne wrote *From the Earth to the Moon*. And H.G. Wells wrote one of the most famous works of science fiction: *The War of the Worlds*. It was about a topic that would be common in twentieth-century science fiction:
20 alien **invasions** of the Earth.

The twentieth century saw the popularity of science fiction increase greatly. **❶** Among the greatest science-fiction writers

of the day were Robert Heinlein and Frank Herbert. ❷ Their works were not   *25*
simply **adventure** stories. ❸ Works by Heinlein such as *Starship Troopers*
and *The Moon Is a Harsh Mistress* introduced **political** topics. ❹ And Frank
Herbert's *Dune* stressed the importance of the environment.

Many popular science-fiction works were turned into movies. Movies
such as *Star Wars* and *Avatar* helped the genre become more popular. In   *30*
more recent times, *Iron Man*, *The Avengers*, and other **superhero** movies
have made science fiction more popular than ever before.   **Words 284**

P5 How _____
helped the genre become
more popular

 Check what the passage is mainly about.

a. The development of science fiction as a genre

b. Reasons why people like reading science fiction

c. The most popular works of science fiction

d. The most famous authors of science-fiction books

i There are both hard science
fiction and soft science
fiction. Hard science
fiction stresses hard
sciences such as physics
and chemistry as well as
technology. Soft science
fiction is more focused on
culture and stories about
people.

Reading Comprehension

1 Which of the following is true about Mary Shelley?

   a. She created the first work of science fiction.

   b. Her books were mostly about monsters.

   c. She came up with the term "science fiction."

   d. She was the first person to write about aliens.

2 In paragraph 2, which of the following can be inferred about early science fiction?

   a. It is very realistic.

   b. It is gloomy and dark.

   c. It is bright and humorous.

   d. It is very peaceful and quiet.

3 Why does the author mention *From the Earth to the Moon*?

   a. To provide details about the story

   b. To compare it with *The War of the Worlds*

   c. To name a science-fiction work with a new topic

   d. To give some information about the author's life

4 Where would the following sentence best fit in paragraph 4?

Many writers published huge numbers of books.

   a. ❶   b. ❷   c. ❸   d. ❹

5 The word introduced in the passage is closest in meaning to

   a. met   b. established   c. studied   d. presented

6 What is important in Frank Herbert's *Dune*?

   It stresses _____.

7 What has made science fiction more popular in more recent times?

   _____

Organizing the Passage

Complete the organizer with the phrases in the box.

	Science Fiction
Who Created It	• Mary Shelley ❶_____ in 1818 and created the first work of science fiction.
The Early Years	• Robert Louis Stevenson wrote about ❷_____ in *Strange Case of Dr. Jekyll and Mr. Hyde*. • Jules Verne looked to the stars in writing *From the Earth to the Moon*. • H.G. Wells wrote about ❸_____ in *The War of the Worlds*.
The Twentieth Century and Later	• Robert Heinlein put ❹_____ in his books such as *Starship Troopers* and *The Moon Is a Harsh Mistress*. • ❺_____ stressed the importance of the environment in *Dune*. • ❻_____ made more people know about science fiction.

Frank Herbert   an alien invasion   published *Frankenstein*
political topics   science-fiction movies   a mad scientist

Summarizing the Passage

Use the phrases in the box to complete the summary.

made into movies   other worlds
environmental topics   dangers of science   the first real work

Mary Shelley published *Frankenstein* in 1818 and wrote ❶_____ of science fiction. This is a genre of speculative fiction that focuses on science and technology, aliens, and ❷_____. Writers like Shelley and Robert Louis Stevenson, who wrote *Strange Case of Dr. Jekyll and Mr. Hyde*, wrote about the ❸_____ and technology. Later writers, such as Jules Verne and H.G. Wells, wrote about the stars and alien invasions. In the twentieth century, writers put political and ❹_____ into their works. Many science-fiction stories were ❺_____, which helped science fiction become more popular.

Unit 8

Famous Detectives in Literature

Think about the Topic

1 Who are some famous detectives in literature that you know about?

2 What works of detective fiction are you familiar with? How did you like them?

Vocabulary Preview

A **Match the words with their definitions by writing the correct letters in the blanks.**

1 feature (v.) _____ a. a situation

2 crime _____ b. the act of killing a person

3 murder _____ c. a bad person in a story

4 villain _____ d. an action that is illegal

5 credit (v.) _____ e. to have something as a major part

6 case _____ f. proof that something happened or is true

7 reasoning _____ g. a feeling a person has about a truth or reality

8 evidence _____ h. to say that someone did something good

9 novelist _____ i. a person who writes works of fiction

10 intuition _____ j. the using of logic to solve a problem

B **Choose the words that have similar** (sim.) **or opposite** (opp.) **meanings from the box.**

reason	motivate	hero

1 villain _____ opp.

2 inspire _____ sim.

3 logic _____ sim.

Background Knowledge

Detectives are people who investigate crimes and try to solve them. There are numerous detective novels nowadays, but this genre is fairly new. To create a good work of detective fiction, a writer needs to have a believable crime. There must be clues that allow careful readers to figure out the mystery, and the detective must be an appealing person.

Famous Detectives in Literature

Q

What is each paragraph mainly about?

P1 What _____ stories are

P2 Who C. Auguste Dupin was and what _____ he was in

P3 How Sherlock Holmes _____ his cases

P4 The (methods / effects) used by Hercule Poirot to solve cases

Detective stories are a popular genre in literature. They **feature** a **crime** such as a **murder** or theft, and a detective must solve the crime and catch the **villain**. Three of the numerous detectives in literature <u>stand out above the others</u>.

▲ Edgar Allan Poe

5 C. Auguste Dupin first appeared in the 1841 short story *The Murders in the Rue Morgue*. Dupin was created by Edgar Allan Poe. Poe is widely **credited** for inventing the detective genre. Dupin would later appear
10 in two more short stories: *The Mystery of Marie Rogêt* and *The Purloined Letter*. To solve the **cases**, Dupin uses his intelligence and **reasoning** to get inside the minds of criminals.

15 Dupin inspired many other detectives that authors wrote about soon afterward. Sir Arthur Conan Doyle was one of these authors. He based his detective, Sherlock Holmes, on Poe's creation. Holmes is a highly intelligent man who uses logic to solve mysteries. He also notices small bits of **evidence** and uses them to figure out the problem. He first appeared
20 in 1887 in *A Study in Scarlet*. Doyle would write a total of fifty-six short stories and four novels featuring Holmes. Among the most famous are the stories *The Adventure of the Speckled Band* and *The Adventure of the Blue *Carbuncle*.

A third famous detective is Hercule Poirot. He is the creation of Agatha
25 Christie, one of the bestselling **novelists** ever. Poirot uses logic to solve

▲ Agatha Christie

▲ Sherlock Holmes

some cases. Yet he also relies on **intuition** and feelings. He can solve cases just by getting people to talk to him. They tell him what really happened. Christie wrote more than thirty novels and fifty short stories with Poirot in them. *Death on the Nile* and *Murder on the Orient Express* are two famous ones. **Words 289**

30

i Sherlock Holmes was extremely popular with readers, but Doyle got tired of writing about him, so he had Holmes die in a story. Because so many people became upset, Doyle brought Holmes back and wrote more stories featuring him.

* carbuncle: a type of gemstone

 Check the main point of the passage.

a. Sherlock Holmes is the best-known detective in literature.

b. There are three detectives in fiction that are very famous.

c. Writers of detective stories must have creative minds.

d. Edgar Allan Poe was the first person to write detective fiction.

Reading Comprehension

1 What does the underlined part in the passage mean?

   a. were the first detectives in novels

   b. have never failed to solve a case

   c. are better known than other detectives

   d. use the most interesting methods

2 Which of the following is NOT true about C. Auguste Dupin?

   a. He was created by Edgar Allan Poe.

   b. He first appeared in *The Purloined Letter*.

   c. He used his intelligence and reasoning to solve cases.

   d. He motivated Sir Arthur Conan Dolye to create Sherlock Holmes.

3 The word He in the passage refers to

   a. Dupin

   b. Sir Arthur Conan Doyle

   c. Sherlock Holmes

   d. Poe's creation

4 In paragraph 3, which of the following is mentioned about Sherlock Holmes?

   a. With whom he solve cases

   b. How many cases he solved

   c. When he last appeared in a story

   d. What he notices and uses to solve crimes

5 The phrase relies on in the passage is closest in meaning to

   a. considers   b. trusts   c. desires   d. rejects

6 What is Edgar Allan Poe credited for?

   He is widely _____.

7 What are three things that Hercule Poirot uses to solve cases?

   _____

Organizing the Passage

Select the appropriate statements from the answer choices and match them to the detective to which they relate. Two of the answer choices will NOT be used.

C. Auguste Dupin	Sherlock Holmes	Hercule Poirot
•	•	•
•	•	•
	•	

1 Is able to notice small bits of evidence

2 Can get people to tell him what happened

3 Was created by Edgar Allan Poe

4 Is based on another detective

5 Usually carries a gun when he is on cases

6 Is a character in fifty-six short stories and four novels

7 Has had many movies made based on his stories

8 Appears in "The Murders in the Rue Morgue"

9 Uses logic as well as intuition and feelings to solve cases

Summarizing the Passage

Use the phrases in the box to complete the summary.

> solve a crime   intelligence and reasoning
> intuition and feelings   Agatha Christie   very intelligent

The detective genre involves a person trying to ❶_____. It was created by

Edgar Allan Poe, who wrote "The Murders in the Rue Morgue," which featured C. Auguste

Dupin. Dupin uses ❷_____ to solve crimes. Sir Arthur Conan Doyle based

Sherlock Holmes on Dupin. Holmes is ❸_____ and solves crimes by using small

bits of evidence. ❹_____ put Hercule Poirot into more than thirty novels and fifty

short stories. He uses logic but can also solve cases with ❺_____.

Chapter 5
Zoology

Zoology is the scientific study of animals, including where they live and how they behave. Zoologists study animals to learn about their relationships with the environment and how they affect their ecosystems.

Unit 9
Rediscovered Species

▲ A black-footed ferret

Think about the Topic

1 Why do you think some species of animals get lost?

2 What can cause an animal to become extinct?

Vocabulary Preview

A **Match the words with their definitions by writing the correct letters in the blanks.**

1 billion _____ a. very small

2 species _____ b. no longer living

3 extinct _____ c. to disappear, often suddenly

4 rule (v.) _____ d. a group of creatures living together

5 prehistoric _____ e. 1,000,000,000; one thousand million

6 tiny _____ f. relating to the time before writing

7 colony _____ g. to control an area by being the strongest

8 diet _____ h. food that a person or animal eats each day

9 vanish _____ i. to look around a new place to discover something

10 explore _____ j. a group of plants, animals, or other creatures having similar characteristics

B **Choose the words that have similar** (*sim.*) **or opposite** (*opp.*) **meanings from the box.**

shore	appear	connection

1 vanish _____ *opp.*

2 coast _____ *sim.*

3 link _____ *sim.*

Background Knowledge

Life has existed on the Earth for billions of years, and countless species have appeared and then gone extinct during that time. Natural disasters sometimes cause extinctions. These include volcanic eruptions, tsunamis, floods, and even asteroid strikes on the planet. In modern times, hunting, deforestation, and pollution—all caused by humans—have resulted in animals going extinct.

Rediscovered Species

Q

What is each paragraph mainly about?

P1 What has happened to many (species / years) on the Earth

P2 The _____ and why it is a rediscovered species

P3 Two other rediscovered species: the gracilidris and the _____

Scientists believe that life has existed on the Earth for at least 3.8 **billion** years. During that time, countless numbers of **species** have lived and then gone **extinct**. The dinosaurs are the most famous extinct animals. ❶ For tens of millions of years, they **ruled** the Earth. ❷ This has happened to other
5 animals as well. ❸ But people may find animals they once thought were extinct to be alive. ❹ These are called rediscovered species.

The dinosaurs are not rediscovered species since nobody has found any alive today. Yet at least one animal that lived during the time of the dinosaurs is a rediscovered species. This is the coelacanth. It was a
10 **prehistoric** fish that lived millions of years ago. Scientists considered it a missing link between fish and animals that could walk on land. For the longest time, they thought it had gone extinct sixty-five million years ago. That was when the dinosaurs died out. But in 1938, a living coelacanth was found off the coast of South Africa.

15 A smaller example than the two-meter-long coelacanth is the gracilidris. This is a **tiny** species of ant. It disappeared from the *fossil record fifteen million years ago. Then, in 2006, living gracilidris **colonies** were found

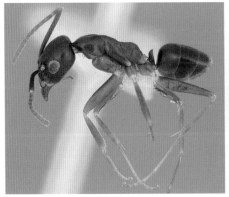

▴ Gracilidris

▴ Laotian rock rat

▲ Coelacanth

in South America. Another animal, the Laotian rock rat, was thought to have gone extinct ten million years ago. Scientists rediscovered it in 2005. Various tribes in Laos were already aware it existed though. They often included it in their **diets**.

20

There are many other examples of rediscovered species. Some **vanished** millions of years ago. Others disappeared only hundreds of years ago. As people **explore** more places around the world, they will likely find even more animals once thought to be dead. Words 289

Q4 (Where / What) will likely happen regarding rediscovered species in the future

*fossil record: all the fossils that have been found and the information learned from them

i The coelacanth may help scientists understand how animals moved from the sea to land. It is not a direct ancestor of land-living creatures with four legs. However, by studying the coelacanth, scientists can learn more about the transition to land animals made millions of years ago.

Check the main point of the passage.

a. It is common for rediscovered species to go extinct for many years.

b. The dinosaurs used to be considered rediscovered species.

c. Most animals that have lived on the Earth are no longer alive.

d. Some animals once thought to be extinct have been found alive.

Reading Comprehension

1 Where would the following sentence best fit in paragraph 1?

Then, they suddenly all died.

   a. ❶   b. ❷   c. ❸   d. ❹

2 Which of the following is NOT true about the coelacanth?

   a. People used to believe it was extinct.

   b. It is smaller in size than most other fish.

   c. It is a fish that lived when dinosaurs were alive.

   d. The fish was found alive near South Africa in 1938.

3 In paragraph 3, which of the following is NOT mentioned about the gracilidris?

   a. When it disappeared

   b. Where it was rediscovered

   c. What kind of species it is

   d. Who found the species

4 What does the underlined part in the passage mean?

   a. They often hunted it.

   b. They often ate it.

   c. They often raised it.

   d. They often saw it.

5 Which of the following can be inferred about rediscovered species?

   a. They are some of the world's most famous animals.

   b. Most of them are found in the world's oceans.

   c. There will probably be more of them in the future.

   d. It has been a long time since a new one has been found.

6 Why are dinosaurs not considered a rediscovered species?

Nobody has _____.

7 What did scientists think about the coelacanth?

_____

Organizing the Passage

Select the appropriate statements from the answer choices and match them to the rediscovered species to which they relate. Two of the answer choices will NOT be used.

Coelacanth	Gracilidris	Laotian Rock Rat
•	•	•
•	•	•

1 Is eaten by some tribes in Laos

2 Is considered a type of dinosaur by scientists

3 Was found in South America in 2006

4 Was rediscovered by people in the early nineteenth century

5 Is an ant thought to have died out fifteen million years ago

6 Was thought to have gone extinct with the dinosaurs but was found in 1938

7 Was discovered in 2005 after being thought to have gone extinct ten million years ago

8 Was a prehistoric fish considered a missing link between fish and animals that could walk

Summarizing the Passage

Use the phrases in the box to complete the summary.

sixty-five million	found alive
to have vanished in South America	going extinct

Species have been ❶_____ for the past 3.8 billion years. But sometimes animals thought to be extinct are ❷_____. These are rediscovered species. One, the coelacanth, was found in 1938 after people thought it had died out ❸_____ years ago. People also believed the gracilidris, a tiny ant, and the Laotian rock rat had gone extinct. But they were found ❹_____ and Laos, respectively. Some rediscovered species are thought to have died millions of years ago while others are believed ❺_____ a short time ago.

Unit 10

Beavers: Keystone Species

Think about the Topic

1 How do beavers make dams across streams and small rivers?

2 How could the land and animals be affected positively by a beaver dam?

Vocabulary Preview

A **Match the words with their definitions by writing the correct letters in the blanks.**

1 pest _____ a. to fall apart completely

2 semiaquatic _____ b. very wet and covered with water

3 swampy _____ c. an area where animals go to mate

4 ecosystem _____ d. living in or growing close to the water

5 collapse _____ e. to do very well and to be successful

6 endangered species _____ f. an animal that is considered an annoyance

7 breeding ground _____ g. to break down due to the water, wind, or ice

8 erode _____ h. something that makes the air, land, or water dirty

9 pollutant _____ i. an area and all the living and nonliving things in it

10 thrive _____ j. a plant or animal that may not exist for much longer

B **Choose the words that have similar** (*sim.*) **or opposite** (*opp.*) **meanings from the box.**

important	destroy	prosper

1 thrive _____ *sim.*

2 vital _____ *sim.*

3 construct _____ *opp.*

Background Knowledge

The beaver is a large rodent that lives in Europe and North America. It has large front teeth, which it uses to chew trees and other plants. Its diet consists mostly of leaves, roots, and the bark of trees. The beaver has poor eyesight but good hearing, smell, and a sense of touch. It can swim well and can live for up to twenty-four years in the wild.

Beavers:
Keystone Species

Q

What is each paragraph mainly about?

P1 The _____ created by beavers and how people have regarded beavers

P2 (When / Why) keystone species are important

P3 How beavers contribute to their _____

For centuries, people regarded beavers as **pests**. Beavers are **semiaquatic** mammals known mostly for building dams across streams, creeks, and rivers. These dams then create marshes or **swampy** areas behind them. They also stop the flow of water. For these reasons, people
5 have long hunted beavers. In fact, people killed so many of them that they disappeared from numerous regions.

Yet beavers are making a comeback these days. Biologists have realized that rather than being pests, beavers are actually quite helpful. They are so vital that scientists consider beavers to be keystone species. This
10 refers to an animal that is of great importance to its **ecosystem**. In fact, if a keystone species disappeared, its ecosystem would **collapse**.

There are several reasons beavers are keystone species. First, when they dam flowing water, they create new ecosystems. Countless fish, birds, mammals, and other animals live in the wetlands beavers make. Large
15 numbers of them are also **endangered species**. So beavers provide these animals with homes. They often use the wetlands as **breeding grounds** as well. Beavers thus help other species reproduce and increase in number.

▼ A wetland created by a beaver dam

74

The dams that beavers construct provide several benefits, too. By slowing down the flow of water, the dams prevent the surrounding land from **eroding**. When there are heavy rains, the dams can stop floods from occurring or reduce their effects. Finally, beaver dams can remove **pollutants** from flowing water. When various pollutants reach the dams, they get stopped and then cannot head downstream.

Now that people see beavers as keystone species, efforts to introduce them to areas are being made. No longer are beaver dams seen as nuisances. Instead, they are signs that an ecosystem is healthy and **thriving**. Words 282

P4 The (benefits / pollutants) that beaver dams provide the land

20

25

i Beavers have very large front teeth, which they use to bite trees to cut them down. They then place these trees into slow-moving water to block it. They use stones, branches, grass, leaves, and mud to strengthen the dams they build.

 Check the main point of the passage.

a. People have nearly caused beavers to go extinct due to hunting them.

b. The dams that beavers built can create marshes that other animals live in.

c. Beavers are important creatures that benefit the land and other animals.

d. Some people think beavers are pests, but beavers do not harm people.

Reading Comprehension

1 The word them in the passage refers to

   a. streams, creeks, and rivers

   b. these dams

   c. marshes

   d. swampy areas

2 Which of the following can be inferred about beavers?

   a. They are pests that cause great harm to farmers.

   b. There are more today than there were a few years ago.

   c. Scientists always considered them important to their ecosystems.

   d. They are the largest animals to live both on the land and in the water.

3 In paragraph 3, which of the following is mentioned about beavers?

   a. What species of fish live near their dams

   b. How many endangered species they help

   c. Why beavers build dams across water

   d. How their dams help animals reproduce

4 According to paragraph 4, which of the following is NOT true about beaver dams?

   a. They help make the water clean.

   b. They keep water from moving too fast.

   c. They stop floods from happening.

   d. They allow the land to erode.

5 The word nuisances in the passage is closest in meaning to

   a. bothers   b. disadvantages   c. warnings   d. structures

6 What do the dams beavers make create behind them?

   They create _____ .

7 What is a keystone species?

   _____

Organizing the Passage

Complete the organizer with the phrases in the box.

	Beavers: Keystone Species
What Beavers Do	• They build dams across ❶_____. • The dams create marshes or swampy areas and ❷_____ of water.
How They Are Keystone Species	• Their dams create ❸_____. • Fish, birds, mammals, and other animals live in the wetlands they make. • Many animals use the areas as ❹_____.
How Their Dams Help	• They help stop the land from eroding by ❺_____ flowing water. • They can reduce the effects of floods or stop them from happening. • They ❻_____ from flowing water.

stop the flow	slowing down	breeding grounds
remove pollutants	streams, creeks, and rivers	new ecosystems

Summarizing the Passage

Use the phrases in the box to complete the summary.

	endangered species	kill beavers	
introducing beavers		keystone species	prevent erosion

People used to ❶_____ because of the dams they built across streams and rivers. However, beavers are making a comeback because scientists now know they are ❷_____. These are animals that are important to their ecosystems. Beaver dams create new ecosystems that many kinds of animals live in. Some are even ❸_____. They use the areas around the dams as breeding grounds. In addition, beaver dams ❹_____ and stop floods. They also remove pollutants from water. For these reasons, people have started ❺_____ to areas.

Chapter 6

Marketing

Marketing is the act of attempting to convince customers to purchase certain goods or services. Marketers come up with ideas to increase sales at businesses by promoting goods and services in a wide variety of ways.

Marketing

Unit 11
Memorable Commercials

Think about the Topic

1 What are some commercials that you remember?

2 What makes those commercials so memorable?

Vocabulary Preview

A **Match the words with their definitions by writing the correct letters in the blanks.**

1 compliment _____ a. working well or properly

2 memorable _____ b. to react in a positive way

3 commercial _____ c. related to the eyes or sight

4 marketer _____ d. a picture or image that represents something

5 slogan _____ e. a person who thinks of ways to sell things

6 icon _____ f. to tell the public about a product to try to sell it

7 effective _____ g. easy to remember because something is enjoyable

8 advertise _____ h. an advertisement that appears on TV or the radio

9 respond _____ i. to make nice or positive comments about something

10 visual _____ j. a phrase used by a person or group to attract attention

B **Choose the words that have similar** (*sim.*) **or opposite** (*opp.*) **meanings from the box.**

unforgettable	rabbit	young

1 bunny _____ *sim.*

2 elderly _____ *opp.*

3 memorable _____ *sim.*

Background Knowledge

In 1941, the first TV commercial aired. It was an ad for a watch. The company paid $9 to show the ad. Nowadays, commercials cost thousands of dollars to air. For some sporting events, a thirty-second ad can cost several million dollars. Companies purchase commercial time on television because it is an effective way to sell goods and services.

Memorable Commercials

Q

What is each paragraph mainly about?

P1 (When / Why) a commercial for Wendy's became famous

P2 The importance of a _____ in creating a memorable ad

P3 Some famous examples of _____ used in commercials

Two women look at a hamburger and **compliment** it. Another elderly woman takes a look. She asks, "Where's the beef?" after seeing how small the burger is. The woman was Clara Peller, and she was in an ad for the fast-food chain Wendy's. The 1984 ad would become one of the most

5 **memorable commercials** in history.

Marketers are always trying to create memorable ads. There are several ways to do this. One is to create a tagline—or **slogan**—that people remember. "Where's the beef?" is one of these. "Just do it," the tagline

10 for Nike, is another. Nike used that slogan to _____ millions of the Air Jordan basketball sneakers worn by Michael Jordan in the 1980s and 1990s. "Have a Coke and a smile" was introduced in 1979. It helped make several memorable commercials for Coca-Cola.

15 Using **icons** is another way to make **effective** commercials. The Energizer Bunny is among the most famous icons. This toy rabbit, which is powered by Energizer batteries, keeps going when other toys using different batteries have stopped. Starting in 1988, the Energizer Bunny

appeared in more than 100 commercials for eight years. Tony the Tiger is a
memorable icon for a breakfast cereal made by Kellogg's. The Pringles Guy, ²⁰
who **advertises** potato chips, and the M&M chocolates, which advertise
candy, are two other icons in memorable ads.

Humor can create many memorable ads. People often **respond** well to
visual humor. Funny ads may show people falling down, animals doing
various activities like people, and people telling jokes. Yet marketers have ²⁵
learned an interesting fact. While people remember funny ads, they often
forget the products. So marketers who want to create ads that people
remember frequently avoid humor. Words 285

P4 The effect of (humor /
marketers) on ads

 Check what the passage is mainly about.

a. How to come up with an ideal tagline

b. Methods marketers use to sell products in stores

c. The importance of icons when making advertisements

d. Some ways marketers create memorable commercials

i In 1984, Clara Peller
became one of the most
famous women in the
United States. Peller, who
was in her eighties, had a
unique voice and manner
that made her appeal to
people. Thanks to her,
sales at Wendy's increased
dramatically.

Reading Comprehension

1 Why does the author mention Clara Peller?

    a. To compare her commercial with Michael Jordan's

    b. To describe her role in a successful advertisement

    c. To point out how old she was when filming an ad

    d. To explain how she came to appear in an advertisement

2 What is the best choice for the blank?

    a. sell   b. design   c. make   d. sponsor

3 The word powered in the passage is closest in meaning to

    a. stored   b. used   c. created   d. driven

4 In paragraph 3, all of the following questions are answered EXCEPT:

    a. What is appealing about icons to customers?

    b. What kind of product does Tony the Tiger advertise?

    c. What are the Pringles Guy and the M&M chocolates?

    d. How many advertisements did the Energizer Bunny appear in?

5 According to paragraph 4, which of the following is true about humor?

    a. It only works when it is visual humor.

    b. It features in the most profitable commercials.

    c. It is almost always used by marketers these days.

    d. It can cause people to forget which products are being sold.

6 What do "Just do it," "Where's the beef?," and "Have a Coke and a smile" have in common?

They are all _____ for _____ .

7 What does the Energizer Bunny do?

_____

Organizing the Passage

Select the appropriate statements from the answer choices and match them to the type of advertisement to which they relate. Two of the answer choices will NOT be used.

Tagline	Icon	Humor
•	•	•
•	•	•
•		

1 Allowed Coca-Cola to make some memorable commercials

2 Was used to improve sales at the fast-food restaurant Wendy's

3 Has been used to advertise breakfast cereals and snacks

4 Can frequently cause people to forget what is being sold

5 Resulted in some companies losing large amounts of money

6 Was used by Nike to sell millions of Air Jordan basketball sneakers

7 Includes the Energizer Bunny, which advertised batteries for years

8 Is a funny type of advertisement that people often respond well to it

9 Is widely considered the most effective type of advertisement

Summarizing the Passage

Use the phrases in the box to complete the summary.

> effective commercials   in several commercials
> a small hamburger   visual humor   the most memorable

In a famous Wendy's commercial, Clara Peller looks at ❶_____ and asks, "Where's the beef?" This ad is one of ❷_____ in history. Marketers often use taglines to create memorable ads. "Just do it" is a Nike tagline, and "Have a Coke and a smile" is a tagline ❸_____ for Coca-Cola. Icons such as the Energizer Bunny can make ❹_____. Marketers can use ❺_____ in their ads. But people often forget the products being advertised in funny ads, so marketers often avoid using humor.

Unit 12

Marketing through Social Media

Think about the Topic

1 How often do you use social media, and what do you use it for?

2 How do you think that companies use social media as a marketing tool?

Vocabulary Preview

A **Match the words with their definitions by writing the correct letters in the blanks.**

1 update (n.) _____   a. to communicate directly

2 promote _____   b. new news on a current event

3 post _____   c. to make something better

4 link _____   d. money a person or company makes

5 improve _____   e. something that provides a connection

6 profit _____   f. the number of people who visit a website

7 interact _____   g. to put an article or picture on the Internet

8 traffic _____   h. individuals who regularly buy a company's goods

9 go viral _____   i. to become very popular on the Internet suddenly

10 customer base _____   j. to talk about someone or something to make it more popular

B **Choose the words that have similar** (sim.) **or opposite** (opp.) **meanings from the box.**

compliment	remark	negative

1 positive _____ opp.

2 complaint _____ opp.

3 comment _____ sim.

Background Knowledge

The first social media site appeared on the Internet in 1997. Since then, numerous social media sites have been created. Among them are Facebook, Twitter, MySpace, Photobucket, LinkedIn, and Flickr. Marketers quickly learned how to use these sites. Nowadays, most companies have social media sites that are active at promoting their goods and services directly to members of their target audiences.

Marketing through Social Media

Q

What is each paragraph mainly about?

P1 (How / Where) people and businesses use social media

P2 The types of content that businesses can _____ for SMM

P3 How businesses can _____ from SMM

Around the world, social media has become popular. Hundreds of millions of people use Facebook, Instagram, Twitter, and LinkedIn. People use these websites and others to provide **updates** on their personal lives. They let their friends and family members see what they are doing. These
5 days, companies also use social media. For the most part, they **promote** their products to customers.

The term for this is social media marketing (SMM). Businesses use SMM by creating content and by sharing it on social media. For example, they may **post** short articles and updates. Others may make videos promoting
10 their products. And companies often provide **links** and have discussions on social media. These actions can help businesses a great deal. They allow companies to **improve** their sales and **profits**.

One benefit of SMM is that it brings businesses closer to their customers. ❶ This lets them **interact** directly with businesses. ❷ Then,
15 companies can see what they are doing right and wrong. ❸ For instance,

a travel agency that posts pictures of the tours it leads may get positive comments from customers. ❹ But a restaurant that serves food people do not like may get complaints. In both cases, the companies benefit. They learn what their customers like and dislike. So they can improve the quality of their service.

20

Another good point of SMM is that it can let people learn about a business. A company's website may get small amounts of **traffic**. But thousands or millions of people may view a post on Facebook or a tweet on Twitter that **goes viral**. That can increase a company's **customer base**. And that is what every marketer wants to happen. Words 284

P4 How many people may (create / view) posts on SMM

Check the main idea of the passage.

   a. Most businesses around the world have social media sites.

   b. It is important for people to be involved in social media.

   c. Using social media too much can be harmful to people.

   d. Businesses can get many advantages through social media marketing.

i These days, large numbers of small businesses do not even have their own websites. Instead, they rely upon social media sites. This is especially true of Facebook. It is possible to find all kinds of businesses selling goods and services solely on Facebook.

Reading Comprehension

1 Which of the following is NOT mentioned as content that businesses create for SMM?

   a. Posting short articles

   b. Making videos

   c. Providing links and having discussions

   d. Providing updates on their lives

2 The phrase a great deal in the passage is closest in meaning to

   a. everywhere   b. very much   c. a bargain   d. usually

3 Where would the following sentence best fit in paragraph 3?

Customers can post comments and ask questions on social media sites.

   a. ❶   b. ❷   c. ❸   d. ❹

4 The word they in the passage refers to

   a. complaints

   b. both cases

   c. the companies

   d. their customers

5 According to paragraph 4, which of the following is NOT true about SMM?

   a. It can be used to increase a customer base.

   b. It can force companies to make many new posts each day.

   c. It can provide more traffic than a company's website.

   d. It can help large numbers of people learn about a company.

6 According to paragraph 2, how can SMM help companies?

It allows _____.

7 How do companies benefit from the comments from customers on social media sites?

_____

Organizing the Passage

Complete the organizer with the phrases in the box.

Marketing through Social Media

How Businesses Use Social Media Marketing (SMM)	• Companies use social media to ❶_____. • Businesses use SMM to ❷_____ and then share it on social media. • They can post short ❸_____, make videos, provide links, and have discussions.
Benefits of SMM	• Businesses get closer to their customers by ❹_____ with them. • They can respond to both positive and negative comments from their customers and this lets them improve the ❺_____. • People can learn about businesses ❻_____ on Facebook or seeing viral tweets on Twitter and this can increase businesses' customer base.

create content	by viewing posts	articles and updates
quality of their service	interacting directly	promote their products

Summarizing the Passage

The first sentence of a short summary is provided below. Complete the summary by choosing THREE answer choices that express the most important ideas.

Businesses can use social media marketing to benefit them in many ways.

1 Businesses can interact directly with their customers to learn how they feel.

2 Large numbers of people can learn about new businesses by using social media.

3 Hundreds of millions of people around the world use social media.

4 Companies are always trying to come up with ways to improve their profits.

5 Some companies create various types of content on social media to promote their products.

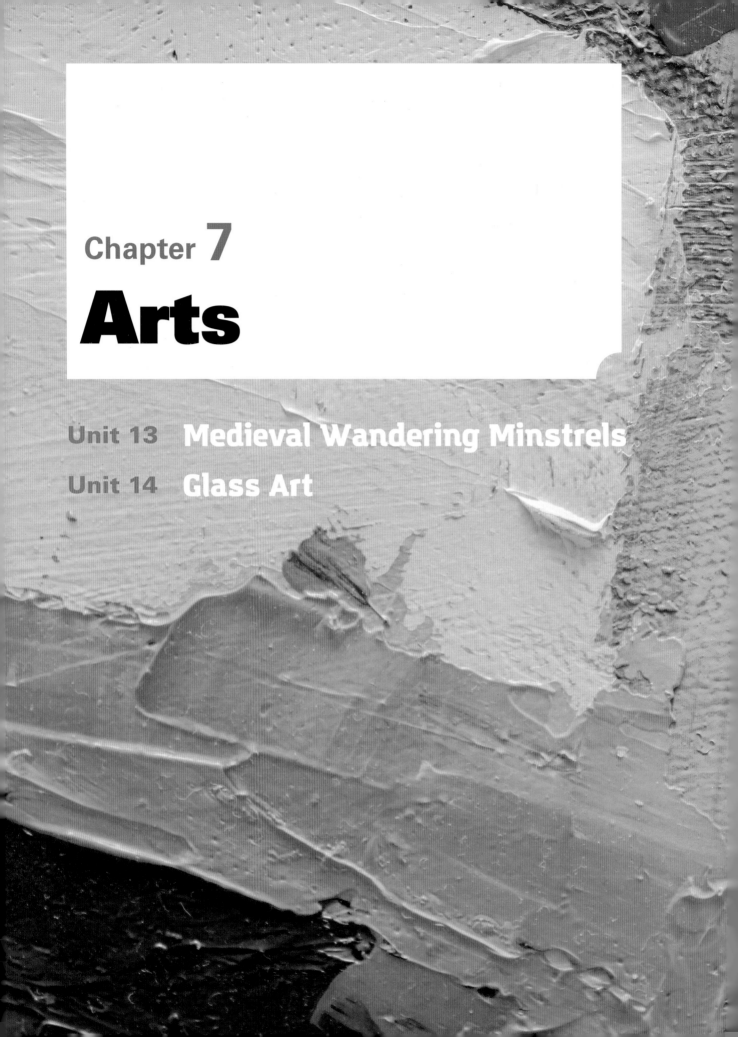

Chapter 7
Arts

The arts refer to the various ways that people express themselves in a creative manner. These include music, writing, art, acting, and dancing. People who are involved in the arts are often imaginative and are good at expressing themselves.

Arts

Unit 13

Medieval Wandering Minstrels

Think about the Topic

1 What do you think life was like in Europe in the Middle Ages?

2 What kind of entertainment did people in the Middle Ages have?

Vocabulary Preview

A **Match the words with their definitions by writing the correct letters in the blanks.**

1 peasant _____ a. a poor farmer

2 feast _____ b. relating to the Middle Ages

3 medieval _____ c. to remember something exactly

4 wandering _____ d. a meal at which there is very much food

5 juggler _____ e. to amuse people or to make them have fun

6 acrobat _____ f. a person skilled at performing difficult acts

7 memorize _____ g. to say aloud the words to a song, book, poem, etc.

8 recite _____ h. traveling from one place to another without a purpose

9 entertain _____ i. a traditional song passed on from one generation to another

10 folksong _____ j. a person able to keep several objects in the air at the same time

B **Choose the words that have similar** (*sim.*) **or opposite** (*opp.*) **meanings from the box.**

skill	worthless	gather

1 ability _____ *sim.*

2 collect _____ *sim.*

3 valuable _____ *opp.*

Background Knowledge

The Middle Ages were a very difficult time for most people. The majority of people during that time were peasants. They did not own the land they farmed. Instead, the local lord owned it. So the peasants owed the lord some of the crops they harvested. Peasants had to work hard all year long, and they had few sources of entertainment.

Medieval Wandering Minstrels

Q

What is each paragraph mainly about?

P1 The types of lives that (peasants / wandering minstrels) lived in the Middle Ages

In Europe during the Middle Ages, there were few forms of entertainment. Regular people, called **peasants**, led hard lives
5 farming the land. For this reason, there were many fairs, festivals, and **feasts** in **medieval** times. These allowed peasants to take a break from working and to
10 enjoy themselves. Among the most popular people at these special events were **wandering** minstrels.

▲ Wandering minstrels

P2 Which (activities / poems) minstrels did

Minstrels were entertainers who were common from the 1100s to the 1600s. Most people today believe that minstrels were just singers. They were much more than that though. They were **jugglers**, dancers,
15 and **acrobats**. They **memorized** poems and stories and **recited** them for crowds. Some performed magic tricks. And others traveled with trained animals and put on shows with them. For all of them, their primary purpose was to **entertain** people.

P3 The types of music minstrels played and

However, it is true that most minstrels are known for their singing
20 and musical abilities. Since they traveled from town to town to perform, minstrels carried light instruments. Most played the lute or the fiddle while others played the harp. As they played their instruments, they often sang. Some made up their own songs. Others performed **folksongs** and ballads popular at the time. Many of their
25 songs and tales had to do with *chivalry and courtly love.

▲ Lute

❶ During the Middle Ages, news traveled very slowly. ❷ As minstrels often moved, they collected news in the many towns they visited. ❸ When they visited other places, they told people about the news they had heard elsewhere. ❹

The wandering minstrels of medieval Europe provided valuable services   30 for people. They not only entertained but also <u>informed others</u>. In doing so, they became some of the most important travelers of their time. **Words 284**

*chivalry: a system that knights followed in the Middle Ages

P4 How minstrels provided people with (entertainment / news)

i Courtly love focuses on chivalry and nobility. Knights were expected to fight for the honor of ladies. They were supposed to behave properly at all times. Ladies were also expected to honor their knights and to be faithful to them.

 Check what the passage is mainly about.

   a. The activities medieval peasants did for entertainment

   b. What life was like for people during the Middle Ages

   c. The manner in which people learned about news in medieval times

   d. The importance of wandering minstrels in medieval society

Reading Comprehension

1 The word **These** in the passage refers to

a. Peasants

b. Hard lives

c. Many fairs, festivals, and feasts

d. Medieval times

2 In paragraph 2, which of the following is NOT mentioned about minstrels?

a. What types of skills they had

b. The purpose of their activities

c. The period when they entertained people

d. The way that they learned their skills

3 Which of the following is true about minstrels according to the passage?

a. They were only entertainers.

b. They had a lot of musical talent.

c. People did not enjoy their performances.

d. They preferred to stay in one place for a long time.

4 Where would the following sentence best fit in paragraph 4?

> Wandering minstrels performed another important service.

a. ❶   b. ❷   c. ❸   d. ❹

5 What does the underlined part in the passage mean?

a. had good educations

b. acted like teachers

c. let people know about news

d. showed others how to do their tricks

6 What did many festivals and fairs allow peasants to do in medieval times?

They allowed peasants to _____ .

7 What were many of the songs wandering minstrels sang about?

_____

Organizing the Passage

Complete the organizer with the phrases in the box.

Medieval Wandering Minstrels

Who They Were	• ❶_____ from the 1100s to the 1600s. • They were not just singers but were jugglers, ❷_____. • They recited ❸_____ and also performed magic tricks.
Their Musical Abilities and Services	• They played ❹_____ such as the lute, fiddle, or harp. • They sang while they played their instruments. • They sang their own songs or folksongs, and many songs had to do with ❺_____. • They ❻_____ in towns and then told people in other towns about it.

collected news   light instruments   dancers, and acrobats

they were entertainers   poems and stories   chivalry and courtly love

Summarizing the Passage

The first sentence of a short summary is provided below. Complete the summary by choosing THREE answer choices that express the most important ideas.

> Wandering minstrels provided several valuable services for people in medieval times.

1 The lives of most peasants in the Middle Ages were very difficult.

2 It was common for wandering minstrels to sing songs and to play musical instruments.

3 Wandering minstrels entertained people with poems, stories, and magic tricks.

4 People often got news from other places from wandering minstrels.

5 The age of the wandering minstrel was from around the 1100s to the 1600s.

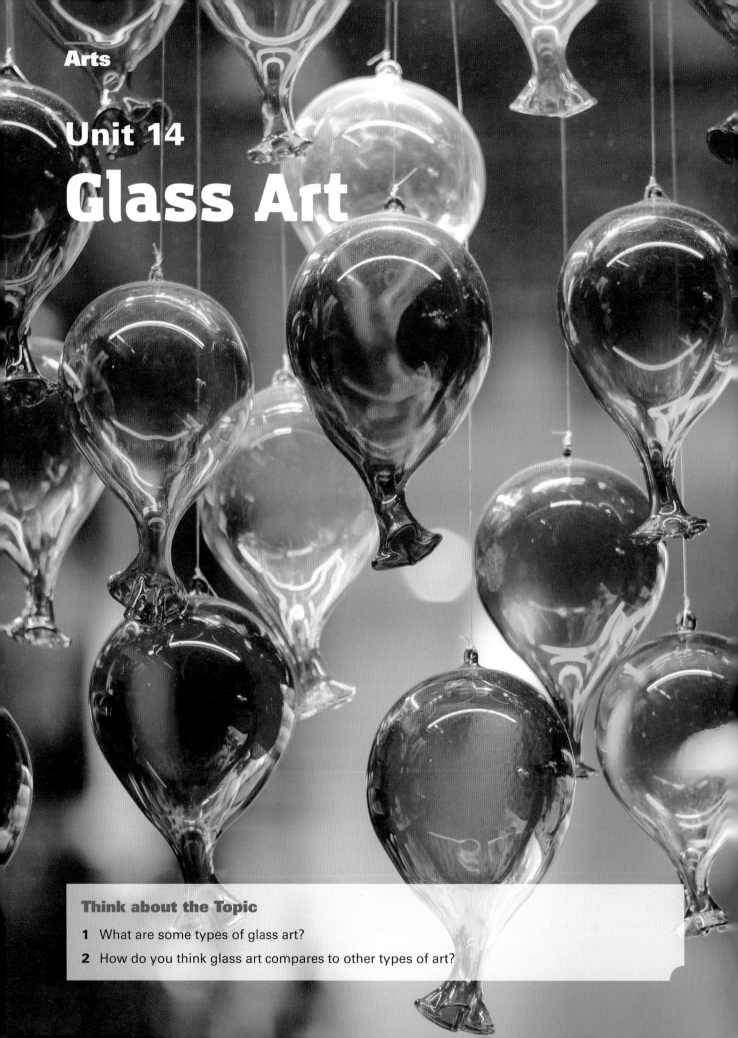

Arts

Unit 14
Glass Art

Think about the Topic

1 What are some types of glass art?

2 How do you think glass art compares to other types of art?

Vocabulary Preview

A Match the words with their definitions by writing the correct letters in the blanks.

1 serve	_____	a.	useful
2 practical	_____	b.	to be useful to; to help
3 bead	_____	c.	the ability to think of new things
4 dig site	_____	d.	standing out more than normal
5 depict	_____	e.	a very large, important church
6 cathedral	_____	f.	to represent something in a picture
7 prominent	_____	g.	to put the parts of something together
8 assemble	_____	h.	a small, round object made of glass, wood, stone, etc.
9 statue	_____	i.	an image of a person or animal made from stone, metal, etc.
10 imagination	_____	j.	a place where archaeologists search for items buried in the ground

B Choose the words that have similar (*sim.*) **or opposite** (*opp.*) **meanings from the box.**

separate	building	look like

1 structure	_____	*sim.*
2 assemble	_____	*opp.*
3 resemble	_____	*sim.*

Background Knowledge

In the past, people learned that they could use glass in a variety of ways. These included using it as jewelry and creating art with it. For thousands of years, people have been coming up with unique ways to create art with glass. Stained-glass windows were popular in medieval times. In modern times, technology allows people to create all kinds of art with glass.

Glass Art

Q

What is each paragraph mainly about?

P1 (Where / How) people have used glass since they started making it

P2 The use of glass as _____ and vases and pots

P3 _____ windows and their uses in the Middle Ages

People have been making glass for around 4,000 years. During that time, it has **served** many purposes. Some are **practical**, such as for making windows and containers. Others are artistic. In fact, people have been making glass art almost since the art of *glassblowing was invented.

5 Archaeologists have dug up glass **beads** at many **dig sites** around the world. Tiny glass beads were worn as jewelry by people everywhere. Another form of glass art was blowing glass into shapes such as vases and pots. Some were created with colored glass while others were decorated after they were completed.

10 The best-known type of glass art is the stained-glass window. Stained-glass windows are made of colored glass and often **depict** images. In Europe in the Middle Ages, stained-glass windows were put in churches and **cathedrals**. They featured images of scenes from the Bible. In a time when _____, the pictures helped explain the Christian religion
15 to people. These windows were so well made that, centuries later, they still exist in many structures.

In more modern times, different kinds of glass art have become **prominent**. Some artists create glass sculptures. They blow glass into different shapes and then **assemble** them into works resembling **statues**. Some artists like to take thick pieces of glass and then use a procedure called sandblasting. This lets them remove parts of the surface of the glass to create sculptures of some type. The artwork created with this method is limited only by the artist's **imagination**. Other individuals create glass art by cutting glass with diamond saws and lasers. Thanks to modern technology, all kinds of beautiful glass art is being created nowadays. **Words 277**

20

P4 Glass art that is made in (modern / ancient) times

*glassblowing: the practice of shaping a piece of hot, melted glass by blowing air through a tube

 Check the main idea of the passage.

a. Glass art results in some beautiful pieces.

b. People can create art with glass in many ways.

c. Modern technology lets people be creative with glass.

d. The art of making glass was learned more than 4,000 years ago.

i Sandblasting requires the use of a sandblaster. It pushes air and sand through it. They hit the surface of the glass and then create pictures.

Reading Comprehension

1 Which of the following is NOT true according to paragraphs 1 and 2?

   a. People wore glass beads as jewelry.
   b. People made vases and pots by blowing glass.
   c. Most people preferred to make glass for artistic reasons.
   d. People learned how to make glass about 4,000 years ago.

2 What is the best choice for the blank?

   a. few people could read
   b. religion was not important
   c. glass was expensive
   d. art was fairly uncommon

3 In paragraph 3, all of the following questions are answered EXCEPT:

   a. What do stained-glass windows usually show?
   b. How did glassmakers create stained-glass windows?
   c. Where did people put stained-glass windows in the past?
   d. What did the pictures in stained-glass windows explain to people?

4 The word procedure in the passage is closest in meaning to

   a. version   b. method   c. tool   d. paint

5 According to paragraph 4, which of the following is true about modern glass art?

   a. It does not use the art of glassblowing anymore.
   b. It is simpler and more practical than art in the past.
   c. Artists prefer to make sculptures than other types of artwork.
   d. Artists use various tools and techniques to create glass art.

6 How do some artists cut glass nowadays to create art glass?

   They cut glass with _____.

7 How do artists create glass sculptures?

   _____

Organizing the Passage

Complete the organizer with the phrases in the box.

Glass Art

The Uses of Glass	• People learned to make glass around 4,000 years ago. • They made it for ❶_____ as well as for artistic reasons.
Glass Art in the Past	• People used ❷_____ as jewelry and blew glass into shapes such as ❸_____. • Stained-glass windows are made of ❹_____ and show images of scenes ❺_____. • They were in churches and cathedrals in Europe in the Middle Ages.
Modern Glass Art	• Artists blow glass into different shapes and put the pieces together to resemble statues. • Some artists ❻_____ to remove parts of the surface of glass to make sculptures. • Artists may cut glass with diamond saws and lasers.

practical reasons	from the Bible	use sandblasting
vases and pots	colored glass	glass beads

Summarizing the Passage

Use the phrases in the box to complete the summary.

featured scenes	churches and cathedrals
create glass sculptures	best-known type	art of glassblowing

Since people invented the ❶_____, they have been making glass art. Some people made glass beads as jewelry while others blew glass into vases and pots that they then decorated. Stained-glass windows are the ❷_____ of glass art. They were found in ❸_____ in Europe in the Middle Ages. They ❹_____ from the Bible. In modern times, some artists ❺_____. Others use sandblasting to remove parts of the surface of glass to create sculptures. Others cut glass with diamond saws and lasers to make glass art.

Chapter 8

Meteorology

Meteorology is the scientific study of the atmosphere, including the weather and the climate. Meteorologists study the atmosphere to learn how it affects the Earth and also to predict the weather in the future.

Unit 15

Tropical Cyclones

Think about the Topic

1 What causes storms to form, and why do they become so powerful?

2 What do you think makes storms move the way they do and affect certain places?

Vocabulary Preview

A **Match the words with their definitions by writing the correct letters in the blanks.**

1 violent	_____	a. basically
2 essentially	_____	b. to reach land
3 make landfall	_____	c. away from the sea or ocean
4 tremendous	_____	d. acting with great power or force
5 destruction	_____	e. great in size, amount, or intensity
6 equator	_____	f. to move in a circular or twisting motion
7 swirl	_____	g. the act of causing damage to something
8 condense	_____	h. to change from a gas to a liquid in form
9 inland	_____	i. the rising of water to go over land it does not usually flow on
10 flooding	_____	j. the imaginary line that runs through the center of the Earth in an east-west direction

B **Choose the words that have similar** (*sim.*) **or opposite** (*opp.*) **meanings from the box.**

dry	strengthen	circumstance

1 condition _____ *sim.*

2 moist _____ *opp.*

3 weaken _____ *opp.*

Background Knowledge

Air pressure measures the weight of the air in the atmosphere. There are both high-pressure systems and low-pressure systems. When cold air pushes down, there is a high-pressure system. This usually results in nice, sunny weather. When warm air rises, this creates a low-pressure system. Clouds form, and rain falls when the air pressure is low.

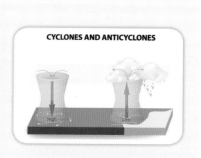

CYCLONES AND ANTICYCLONES

Tropical Cyclones

Q

What is each paragraph mainly about?

P1 What tropical cyclones are and what they are (called / considered)

P2 What _____ tropical cyclones need in order to form

P3 How the (wind / rain) speed of a storm determines what it is called

Tropical cyclones are the world's most **violent** storms. Depending on where they occur, they are called hurricanes, typhoons, and cyclones. But they are **essentially** the same type of storm. When tropical cyclones **make landfall**, they can cause **tremendous** amounts of **destruction**.

5 For a tropical cyclone to form, the proper environmental conditions must exist. First, the ocean's surface temperature must be warm. For this reason, tropical cyclones form in waters relatively close to the **equator**. The warm ocean water heats the air, which gets pushed upward. As the air rises, the area beneath it becomes a low-pressure zone. Air from nearby areas with

10 high air pressure moves into that zone. This happens because the wind blows toward the low-pressure zone. That air then warms, becomes moist, and _____. While it rises, the air begins **swirling**. It also cools off, so the water **condenses**, forming clouds.

The constant spinning and the

15 forming of clouds create a storm. As the storm rotates faster, an eye forms in its center. This area has very low pressure, and it is clear and calm. The winds in the

20 developing storm then move faster. It becomes a tropical storm when the wind speed reaches sixty-three kilometers per hour. And when the wind reaches

25 speeds of 118 kilometers per hour, it becomes a tropical cyclone.

The winds push the storm across the ocean. ❶ When the storm reaches land, it drops enormous amounts of rain. ❷ However, the farther **inland** it goes, the less powerful it gets, so the storm eventually weakens and disappears. ❸ But that usually happens after the rain has caused **flooding** and the high winds have caused great damage. ❹ Words 290

30

P4 What happens to tropical cyclones as they (form / move)

 Check what the passage is mainly about.

  a. Why the eye of a tropical cyclone is so calm

  b. How tropical cyclones form and move

  c. Where tropical cyclones are the most likely to form

  d. The amount of damage tropical cyclones can cause

i Tropical cyclones in the Atlantic Ocean and the eastern Pacific Ocean are called hurricanes. Those in the western Pacific Ocean are called typhoons. And ones in the Indian Ocean are cyclones.

Reading Comprehension

1 According to the passage, which of the following is mentioned about tropical cyclones?

a. The amount of time they usually last

b. The name of ocean they most usually form

c. The various names that people call them

d. In what ways they can cause damage to structures

2 The word it in the passage refers to

a. the warm ocean water   b. the air

c. the area   d. a low-pressure zone

3 What is the best choice for the blank?

a. cools down

b. releases rain

c. starts to go up

d. becomes a high-pressure zone

4 Where would the following sentence best fit in paragraph 4?

> The storm gains power by collecting more and more water from the ocean beneath it.

a. ❶   b. ❷   c. ❸   d. ❹

5 Which of the following is true according to paragraphs 3 and 4?

a. Strong winds blow in the eye of a storm.

b. Tropical cyclones disappear as soon as they reach land.

c. Water from the ocean pushes the storm across the ocean.

d. A tropical cyclone is more powerful than a tropical storm.

6 What happens when warm ocean water heats the air?

The air _____.

7 According to paragraph 3, how does a storm form?

_____

Organizing the Passage

Complete the organizer with the phrases in the box.

	Tropical Cyclone
Where It Forms	• It forms in warm water ❶_____ .
How It Forms	• Air is heated and ❷_____ , and it creates a low-pressure zone. • Air from a high-pressure zone moves in the low-pressure zone. • The air gets warm and moist and rises. • Then, the air cools off, and ❸_____ and forms clouds. • The spinning of the air and the forming of clouds create a storm, and it ❹_____ . • When the wind speed reaches 118km/hr, it becomes a tropical cyclone.
How It Moves and Disappears	• The storm collects water as the wind pushes it ❺_____ . • The storm drops huge amounts of rain on land and weakens as ❻_____ .

water condenses	it heads inland	rotates faster
near the equator	across the ocean	moves upward

Summarizing the Passage

Use the phrases in the box to complete the summary.

	blow fast enough	violent storms
clouds form	gains strength	high-pressure zones

  Tropical cyclones are ❶_____ that form in warm water near the equator. When air gets heated, it rises and forms a low-pressure zone. Air from ❷_____ moves in, where it gets warm and moist and then rises. The air swirls, and ❸_____ , creating a storm. When the storm's winds ❹_____ , it becomes a tropical cyclone. The storm moves across the ocean and ❺_____ by taking in water from the ocean below. When it goes onto land, it rains heavily and causes damage and flooding.

Unit 16

How Ice Ages Occur

Think about the Topic

1 What do you think causes ice ages to occur?

2 Are there any conditions that make ice ages more likely to happen?

Vocabulary Preview

A **Match the words with their definitions by writing the correct letters in the blanks.**

1 undergo _____ a. to find or recognize

2 extreme _____ b. to experience something

3 polar cap _____ c. to go down, often quickly

4 major _____ d. to explode, often violently

5 decline _____ e. far from being normal or average

6 identify _____ f. a round or series that repeats itself

7 cycle _____ g. great in amount, importance, size, etc.

8 orbit (n.) _____ h. any gases that cause the warming of the air

9 greenhouse gas _____ i. the large mass of ice found at each of the Earth's poles

10 erupt _____ j. the path an object takes as it goes around another one

B **Choose the words that have similar (sim.) or opposite (opp.) meanings from the box.**

	absorb	worldwide	closer

1 global _____ sim.

2 farther _____ opp.

3 release _____ opp.

Background Knowledge

Ice ages have been happening for millions of years. The ice sheets that form during ice ages can be several kilometers thick. As they move forward and backward, they are so heavy that they can change the face of the ground beneath them. For instance, they can destroy mountains and create lakes.

How Ice Ages Occur

Q

What is each paragraph mainly about?

P1 (How / Why) the Earth's climate changes over time

P2 The _____ that have occurred on the Earth

P3 How the _____ and the Earth's orbit can cause ice ages

The Earth's climate is constantly **undergoing** changes. However, these normally take place extremely slowly and can only be detected over periods of thousands of years. The global temperature is one way the Earth changes. At times, the Earth endures periods of **extreme** cold, and the ice

5 at its **polar caps** expands greatly. These times are called ice ages.

Throughout Earth's existence, there have been five **major** ice ages. One lasted for more than 200 million years. The shortest ice age, called the Quaternary Ice Age, started 2.5 million years ago and is still going on. These ice ages are not constant periods of coldness though. There are

10 usually long periods of time when temperatures rise, and then they **decline** again later. Right now, the Earth is going through an interglacial period. This means it is in a warm time between very cold periods.

Scientists have **identified** several reasons ice ages occur. A primary cause is the sun. The sun creates energy in **cycles**. When it produces less

15 energy, the Earth's temperature declines. There is sometimes so little energy that the planet enters an ice age. The Earth's orbit can cause ice ages, too. Sometimes the Earth's orbit takes it close to the sun, which results in warm

20 weather. But when the Earth's orbit is farther from the sun, the temperature becomes much colder.

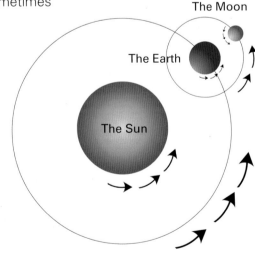

The Earth's Orbit

The Earth's atmosphere can produce ice ages, too. When there are few **greenhouse gases** such as carbon dioxide, the planet can cool. Another cause of ice ages is volcanoes. When they **erupt**, they release large amounts of carbon dioxide into the atmosphere, thereby warming it. But when there are few volcanic eruptions, the Earth's temperature can decline. Words 280

P4 How the Earth's (soil / atmosphere) and volcanoes can cause ice ages

25

> *i* During interglacial periods, the temperature becomes warmer. These times can last for thousands of years. Sea levels tend to rise during them because ice sheets melt. This puts more water into the Earth's oceans, so their water levels rise.

 Check what the passage is mainly about.

a. The effects of ice ages on the Earth

b. The ways that ice ages can come to an end

c. The conditions on the planet during ice ages

d. The reasons that some ice ages take place

Reading Comprehension

1 In paragraph 1, the author implies that the Earth's climate

   a. cannot be observed changing quickly

   b. tends to stay the same every year

   c. is greatly affected by the actions of humans

   d. has caused many species of animals to go extinct

2 The word they in the passage refers to

   a. 2.5 million years ago

   b. constant periods of coldness

   c. long periods of time

   d. temperatures

3 According to paragraph 2, which of the following is true about the Quaternary Ice Age?

   a. It has not yet come to an end.

   b. It lasted longer than all other ice ages.

   c. It took place for 200 million years.

   d. It has been a period of constant coldness.

4 According to paragraphs 3 and 4, which of the following is NOT true about ice ages?

   a. The lack of energy from the sun can cause them.

   b. The longest ones happen due to the Earth's orbit.

   c. Few volcanic eruptions around the Earth can cause them.

   d. The Earth's orbit may be responsible for starting them.

5 The word atmosphere in the passage is closest in meaning to

   a. oxygen   b. gas   c. air   d. climate

6 How many major ice ages has the Earth had?

   The Earth has had _____ .

7 What happens when the Earth's orbit is far from the sun?

   _____

Organizing the Passage

Complete the organizer with the phrases in the box.

How Ice Ages Occur	
How the Climate Changes	• It changes slowly over thousands of years. • There can be times of extreme cold when ❶_____ expand.
How Ice Ages Act	• There have been five major ice ages in the Earth's history. • The Quaternary Ice Age started ❷_____ and is still going on. • There are ❸_____ when the temperature is warmer than the cold times.
Why Ice Ages Occur	• The sun produces less energy, so the temperature declines. • ❹_____ is farther from the sun, so the temperature becomes much colder. • An atmosphere with few ❺_____ can cause cooling to occur. • A lack of ❻_____ can release small amounts of carbon dioxide into the atmosphere.

the polar caps	the Earth's orbit	2.5 million years ago
volcanoes erupting	interglacial periods	greenhouse gases

Summarizing the Passage

The first sentence of a short summary is provided below. Complete the summary by choosing THREE answer choices that express the most important ideas.

> Ice ages are extremely cold periods of time that happen for various reasons.

1 The distance of the Earth to the sun can affect the Earth's temperature.

2 Some volcanoes can erupt and shoot large amounts of greenhouse gases into the air.

3 During ice ages, the global temperature declines greatly, and ice at the polar caps expands.

4 A lack of energy produced by the sun can make the Earth's temperature decline.

5 There is an ice age that is still going on but is currently in an interglacial period.

TOEFL
Practice Test

Medieval Guilds

In Europe in the eleventh century, there was a gradual rise of towns that led to the expanding of trade. Accompanying this development was the establishing of guilds. These were associations composed of all the workers in a particular trade. During medieval times, there were merchant guilds and craft guilds.

Merchant guilds were groups of merchants in a town or region of a country. They were first formed to protect their members from thieves. At the time, Europe was mostly lawless, so transporting goods was dangerous. ■ Merchants thus combined their resources to protect trade routes. ■ Over time, these guilds became wealthy and powerful. ■ They could then set standards for the buying and selling of various goods in a town or region. ■

Craft guilds consisted of all the workers in a particular craft. There were guilds for weavers, blacksmiths, carpenters, bakers, potters, tailors, and shoemakers. Craft guilds set standards of workmanship for their members. These ensured that high-quality goods were being made by their members.

Becoming a member of a guild was not easy. In each town, master craftsmen controlled the guilds. They did not want too many members since that would lessen the amount of work and profits of the guilds' members. So they limited the number of masters in each area. Masters often demanded high fees to train new people in their crafts.

Most trainees started as children and were called apprentices. They worked without pay for many years. As an apprentice became more skilled, he could advance to become a journeyman. This was a paid position. The journeyman then had to complete a special project—a masterpiece—to advance to master craftsman status. After that, he could open his own shop.

1　**In paragraph 2, the author's description of merchant guilds mentions all of the following EXCEPT:**

   (A) Why they were initially created
   (B) How many of them were formed in Europe
   (C) What kinds of people belonged to them
   (D) What type of influence they later had

2 **Look at the four squares [■] that indicate where the following sentence could be added to the passage.**

In fact, many merchants were robbed and even killed while transporting goods.

Where would the sentence best fit?

3 **The word "These" in the passage refers to**

Ⓐ Weavers, blacksmiths, carpenters, bakers, potters, tailors, and shoemakers
Ⓑ Craft guilds
Ⓒ Standards of workmanship
Ⓓ Their members

4 **According to paragraph 4, master craftsmen did not want many members because**

Ⓐ they did not have time to train apprentices
Ⓑ they wanted to do less work
Ⓒ their guilds were fairly small
Ⓓ they wanted to make more money

5 **According to paragraph 5, which of the following is true?**

Ⓐ Most apprentices were paid small amounts of money.
Ⓑ A journeyman could receive money for the work he did.
Ⓒ Only children were allowed to be apprentices.
Ⓓ All journeymen were allowed to have their own shops.

6 **An introductory sentence for a brief summary of the passage is provided below. Complete the summary by selecting the THREE answer choices that express the most important ideas of the passage.**

In the Middle Ages, various guilds were formed for all kinds of workers.

❶ Medieval guilds were able to set standards of production for their members.

❷ A journeyman had to make a masterpiece to become a full guild member.

❸ Some guilds were started to protect their members from thieves.

❹ People had to be trained for years in order to become guild members.

❺ Craft guilds were much more popular than merchant guilds were.

The Layers of a Tropical Rainforest

Tropical rainforests are thick forests with trees growing close to one another. Located near the equator, they grow in Asia, Australia, Africa, and the Americas. They are the most diverse places in the world as biologists estimate they contain about thirty million plant and animal species. Rainforests themselves have different layers, each of which has its own unique characteristics.

The forest floor is the lowest level. It is dark and humid there. So grasses, mosses, and fungi mostly grow in it. It is covered with fallen leaves, seeds, fruits, and branches as well. The largest animals in rainforests live there. These include tigers, elephants, jaguars, and anteaters.

The understory lies above the forest floor. Only a small amount of sunlight can pass the leaves above to reach the understory. Plant life in the understory is limited to young trees, shrubs, and plants that require little light, such as ferns. Mosses and fungi cover the trunks of trees there. Numerous insects live in the understory. Birds, bats, and reptiles such as lizards and snakes live there, too.

The canopy rises around thirty-five meters above the floor. It is the dense roof of the forest. About ninety percent of all life in the forest lives there. The thick leaves make it hard for animals to see others, and the trees are full of various fruits and berries. Insects, mammals such as monkeys, orangutans, birds, and sloths live there.

The emergent layer contains the giant trees that can reach heights of seventy to 100 meters. This layer is the highest, so it receives the most sunlight. It also features high temperatures, high humidity, and strong winds. Monkeys, bats, and all kinds of birds live at the top of the rainforest.

---

1 **The word "diverse" in the passage is closest in meaning to**

Ⓐ studied

Ⓑ remote

Ⓒ dangerous

Ⓓ varied

2   **In paragraph 2, why does the author mention "grasses, mosses, and fungi"?**

Ⓐ To compare them with the ferns in the understory
Ⓑ To name some plants growing on the forest floor
Ⓒ To describe the kinds of fruits they produce
Ⓓ To point out that many animals eat them for food

3   **In paragraph 3, which of the following can be inferred about the understory?**

Ⓐ Many large animals can be found in it.
Ⓑ It receives more light than the forest floor.
Ⓒ Reptiles are the most common animal there.
Ⓓ Tall trees are able to grow well in it.

4   **Which of the following is mentioned about the canopy in paragraph 4?**

Ⓐ What types of fruits and berries grow in it
Ⓑ How many types of trees can be found there
Ⓒ Which kinds of animals dwell in it
Ⓓ Why the trees growing in it have thick leaves

5   **According to paragraph 5, which of the following is NOT true about the emergent layer?**

Ⓐ A variety of animals live in it.
Ⓑ It is the highest level of the rainforest.
Ⓒ It is exposed to large amounts of sunlight.
Ⓓ The weather is cool and dry there.

6   **An introductory sentence for a brief summary of the passage is provided below. Complete the summary by selecting the THREE answer choices that express the most important ideas of the passage.**

> There are four distinct layers in rainforests, and each has its own characteristics.

① Various mammals, birds, insects, and reptiles are found in each layer.

② The lower layers of the rainforest get less sunlight than the upper ones.

③ The largest animals in rainforests live on the forest floor.

④ Rainforests can be dangerous places for most people to visit.

⑤ The amount of light in each layer determines which plants are in it.

From Roman Camp to City

Rome was founded as a small town in 753 B.C. and developed into large, powerful empire. The Romans conquered large areas of Europe, the Middle East, and Asia. They accomplished this feat thanks to their armies, called legions. The legions marched across the Roman Empire to defeat enemies and to keep the peace. Each night, they built camps for defense.

When Roman legions stopped marching for the day, they erected a square-shaped camp with small walls. Each wall had gates, and two roads intersected the camp's interior. Though temporary, these forts were well built and easily defended.

At important locations, these camps became permanent forts with soldiers always stationed in them. This system of forts expanded as the empire grew in size. For instance, in Britain alone, archaeologists have found the remains of more than 400 Roman forts. These forts maintained the empire's control over conquered lands. Some were huge bases that provided supplies for soldiers, and others were on borders near Germany, Scotland, and the Near East. They kept people in the Roman Empire safe from invaders.

The forts attracted people who came to sell their goods to the soldiers. Many legionaries—Roman soldiers—settled by the forts when they retired. Some married local women and raised families, increasing the sizes of the local populations. When the Roman Empire collapsed in the fifth century, there were already towns around many forts.

Over time, some towns developed into cities. Vienna, Austria, started as the Roman fort Vindobona in 15 B.C. Located on the Danube River, it was on Rome's border at the time. The fort Londinium in Britain was founded in 43 A.D. By the second century, it had more than 60,000 people and would later become London, England.

1 **In paragraph 1, why does the author mention "large areas of Europe, the Middle East, and Asia"?**

   Ⓐ To claim they were of great importance to Rome

   Ⓑ To state the areas where the Romans lost wars

   Ⓒ To show where many Roman camps were built

   Ⓓ To name some places where the Romans had land

2 **According to paragraph 2, which of the following is true about the camps the Roman legions erected?**

(A) They were used for a short time.

(B) They had gates only by the roads.

(C) They were not strongly built.

(D) They were made in different shapes.

3 **What is closest in meaning to the word "stationed"?**

(A) attracted

(B) based

(C) reported

(D) trained

4 **Which of the following can be inferred from paragraph 4?**

(A) The Roman Empire no longer existed in the fourth century.

(B) Many legionaries did not return to Rome after retiring.

(C) The legionaries were the best soldiers in the ancient world.

(D) Large numbers of legionaries later became merchants.

5 **In paragraph 5, all of the following questions are answered EXCEPT:**

(A) What was the original name of Vienna, Austria?

(B) Where was Vindobona built?

(C) In what year was Londinium established?

(D) How many people lived in Londinium when it was founded?

6 **An introductory sentence for a brief summary of the passage is provided below. Complete the summary by selecting the THREE answer choices that express the most important ideas of the passage.**

Some camps made by Roman legions were later made into larger places.

① The Roman Empire had to build many forts to protect its borders.

② Some Roman camps became permanent forts that had soldiers in them all the time.

③ Some towns established by the Romans grew to become cities over time.

④ Small towns arose around some forts due to legionaries retiring around them.

⑤ Roman legions were able to build overnight camps in a short amount of time.

The Layers of the Earth

While the Earth appears to be a solid ball of rock, that is not actually true. It has four distinct layers that go from the surface to the center. These layers are the crust, the mantle, the outer core, and the inner core.

The outermost layer is the crust, which extends from the surface to approximately eighty kilometers deep in some places. There are two distinct parts: the continental crust, which includes landmasses, and the oceanic crust, which is located under the oceans. The continental crust is thicker than the oceanic crust. The crust only makes up about one percent of the planet's mass, making it the smallest layer.

The mantle is the thickest and heaviest part of the Earth. It extends from beneath the crust to around 3,000 kilometers deep. The mantle comprises sixty-eight percent of the Earth's total mass and has two separate layers: the upper mantle and the lower mantle. The mantle is very hot, so much of the rock in it is melted. This rock moves very slowly, which causes the crust above it to move as well.

The final layer is the core, which contains the remainder of the Earth's mass. The outer core is about 2,400 kilometers thick and is composed mainly of iron and nickel. Both exist in a liquid state. The outer core is extremely hot with temperatures higher than 4,000 degrees Celsius. Scientists believe the movement of the hot liquid rock there is responsible for creating the Earth's magnetic field. As for the inner core, it is a dense, solid ball of iron and nickel. It has a *radius of 1,200 kilometers and is the planet's hottest part. Temperatures there can rise up to 5,400 degrees Celsius.

*radius: a straight line going from the center of a sphere or circle to the outer part of it

1 **Why does the author mention "the planet's mass"?**
   Ⓐ To compare its mass with another planet's
   Ⓑ To show how heavy landmasses are
   Ⓒ To emphasize the importance of mass
   Ⓓ To point out the size of the crust

2 **Which of the following is true about the mantle?**

(A) It is the largest of the Earth's four layers.

(B) It can be affected by the core beneath it.

(C) Its two parts are mostly made of solid rock.

(D) Its temperature is hotter than that of the core.

3 **The word "dense" in the passage is closest in meaning to**

(A) unique

(B) small

(C) thick

(D) mysterious

4 **In paragraph 4, all of the following questions are answered EXCEPT:**

(A) How hot can the inner core get?

(B) What can be the reason the Earth has a magnetic field?

(C) Why is the outer core thicker than the inner core?

(D) What are the inner core and outer core mostly made of?

5 **Select the appropriate statements from the answer choices and match them to layer of the Earth to which they relate. Two of the answer choices will NOT be used.**

<table>
<tr><td align="center">**STATEMENTS**</td><td align="center">**THE LAYERS OF THE EARTH**</td></tr>
<tr><td>① Has one solid part and one liquid part</td><td>**Crust** (Select 2)</td></tr>
<tr><td>② Has the greatest amount of mass of the Earth's layers</td><td>•
•</td></tr>
<tr><td>③ Is the tiniest of the Earth's layers</td><td></td></tr>
<tr><td>④ Contains the hottest place on the planet</td><td>**Mantle** (Select 2)</td></tr>
<tr><td>⑤ Can make the Earth's magnetic field more powerful</td><td>•
•</td></tr>
<tr><td>⑥ Is directly beneath the oceans</td><td></td></tr>
<tr><td>⑦ Has the most pressure of all three layers</td><td>**Core** (Select 3)</td></tr>
<tr><td>⑧ Is made up of iron and nickel</td><td>•
•
•</td></tr>
<tr><td>⑨ Moves slowly and makes another layer move</td><td></td></tr>
</table>

MEMO

MEMO

MEMO

Building Background Knowledge for Academic Subjects

Fundamental Reading

Workbook

PLUS 1

DARAKWON

Building Background Knowledge for Academic Subjects

Fundamental Reading

Michael A. Putlack
Stephen Poirier
Tony Covello

Workbook

PLUS 1

DARAKWON

Unit 1 Ancient Food Preservation Methods

Vocabulary

A **Read the sentences and choose the best words for the blanks.**

1 The **decay** of food is the process of _____ food slowly.

  a. breaking down b. cooking c. freezing d. drying

2 When it is time for the **harvest**, farmers _____ crops from their fields.

  a. plant b. water c. protect d. gather

3 In ancient times, people hoped to **transform** lead by _____ it into gold.

  a. selling b. mining c. changing d. removing

B **Choose the words from the box to complete the sentences.**

moisture	edible	bacteria	seal	refrigeration

1 _____ can make lots of food go bad very quickly.

2 Food that has been smoked can be _____ for a long time.

3 People can use fat to _____ meat to prevent it from spoiling.

4 Thanks to _____, people can save food for long periods of time.

5 When drying food, a person must make sure there is no _____ left in it.

Translation

C **Read the sentences and translate them into your language.**

1 The cold temperatures froze food, which kept it edible for a long time.

  → _____

2 That enabled them to survive times of drought and bad harvests as well as harsh winters.

  → _____

3 Thousands of years ago, people in ancient times needed to preserve the food they grew, hunted, and caught.

  → _____

Paraphrasing

D **Paraphrase the sentences from the passage with the phrases in the box.**

small pieces	used the weather	keep food good	hot places
could consume	change food	kinds of foods	for taste

1 People often preserved food by taking advantage of the local climate.

→ People often _____ to help them _____.

2 People cut meat or fish into thin strips and then covered it with salt to add flavor.

→ Meat and fish were cut into _____, and then salt was added _____.

3 This process of decay transformed food into something else they could eat or drink.

→ Decay could _____ into something people _____.

4 Individuals living in hot, sunny climates used the sun's heat to dry food such as grains, fruits, vegetables, fish, and meat.

→ In _____, the heat of the sun was able to dry lots of different _____.

Listening

E **Listen to the summary and fill in the blanks.**

People in ancient times came up with many different methods to ❶ _____ food. Those in cold climates ❷ _____ food to keep it edible. Those in hot, sunny climates dried food to remove ❸ _____. Some people ❹ _____ food and ❺ _____ it. Smoking killed bacteria. Sometimes one food was ❻ _____ by another in a process called immersion. People made confit by cooking bird meat in its own ❼ _____. And ❽ _____ decayed food and ❾ _____ it into something else that stayed good for a long time. These methods let people ❿ _____ hard times.

Unit 2 Lost Tribes of the Amazon

Vocabulary

A **Read the sentences and choose the best words for the blanks.**

1 The most **immense** animal is the elephant, which is _____ in size.

    a. average   b. huge   c. tiny   d. normal

2 The hunter improved his **spear** by sharpening the _____ of it.

    a. point   b. blade   c. arrow   d. bow

3 **Loggers** in some forests are _____ too many trees.

    a. planting   b. growing   c. cutting down   d. stealing

B **Choose the words from the box to complete the sentences.**

tribe	ancestors	law	hut	uncontacted

1 The people live in a small _____ in the middle of the jungle.

2 All of the members of the _____ in New Guinea are related to one another.

3 People must obey the _____, or they will be punished in some way.

4 The tribe members still live like their _____ did hundreds of years ago.

5 It is possible to find a few _____ tribes deep in jungles around the world.

Translation

C **Read the sentences and translate them into your language.**

1 The homes of lost tribes are simple huts made of wood and straw.

   → _____

2 Loggers, gold miners, and drug traffickers have been moving into their lands.

   → _____

3 These lost tribes follow the ways of their ancestors, so they lead primitive lives.

   → _____

Paraphrasing

D **Paraphrase the sentences from the passage with the phrases in the box.**

uncontacted people	elderly members	trying to
to have problems	teach the children	South American nations

1 The Amazon Rainforest covers an immense area of land in nine countries in South America.

→ The Amazon Rainforest can be found in nine _____ .

2 Children learn directly from their parents and older members of their communities.

→ Parents and _____ of the community _____ .

3 In recent years, members of lost tribes have suffered at the hands of modern-day people.

→ Modern-day people have caused some tribes _____ recently.

4 The governments of many South American countries are attempting to protect these lost tribes.

→ Many national governments in South America are _____ protect the

_____ .

Listening

E **Listen to the summary and fill in the blanks.**

There are uncontacted ❶ _____ living deep in the Amazon Rainforest in South America. Most of them have had ❷ _____ with the outside world, but they still live ❸ _____ lives. They live in ❹ _____ and wear clothes made of natural materials. They hunt for food. Their educations focus on ❺ _____ in the jungle.

❻ _____ , gold miners, and drug traffickers have been moving into their lands. They sometimes kill tribe members or give them ❼ _____ . Governments have ❽ _____ laws to help them and are ❾ _____ people from entering parts of the rainforest. These let tribe members live in ❿ _____ .

Unit 3 **Mob Mentality**

Vocabulary

A **Read the sentences and choose the best words for the blanks.**

1 Please act with **restraint** and _____ doing anything bad.

a. talk about   b. hold back from   c. consider   d. dislike

2 You should **engage in** the activities and be more _____ them.

a. indifferent to   b. unfriendly to   c. passionate about   d. involved with

3 Her **preference** is for outdoor activities, so she _____ soccer more than video games.

a. likes   b. ignores   c. dislikes   d. knows about

B **Choose the words from the box to complete the sentences.**

enthusiastic	interaction	invisible	rioting	herd

1 The crowd is _____ and is cheering for the speaker.

2 By hiding in the corner, he feels like he is _____ to most people.

3 _____ between others is very important for human relations.

4 Some people prefer to follow the _____ rather than act independently.

5 Hundreds of police officers were required to stop _____ downtown.

Translation

C **Read the sentences and translate them into your language.**

1 Other street riots happen when fans celebrate a sports victory.

→ _____

2 People often make decisions based on personal preferences or by how they can benefit.

→ _____

3 Herd mentality appears in many areas of human interaction and can be violent or nonviolent.

→ _____

Paraphrasing

D Paraphrase the sentences from the passage with the phrases in the box.

not typical	go crazy	becoming violent
they want to	other people	a large number of

1 People give up their own desires and follow those of a larger group.

→ Some people follow a bigger group rather than doing what _____.

2 These terms create images of crowds of people rioting in the streets in most people's minds.

→ These terms make most people think of crowds _____ in the streets.

3 On this day, shoppers often seem to lose their minds by trying to buy as much as they can.

→ Shoppers seem to _____ on this day by buying _____ items.

4 They engage in activities that they would not normally do and simply follow the crowd.

→ They follow _____ and act in a manner that is _____ for them.

Listening

E Listen to the summary and fill in the blanks.

People sometimes engage in mob ❶ _____ or herd mentality. In doing so, they give up their own ❷ _____ and follow those of a larger group. Their actions can be ❸ _____ or nonviolent. Street ❹ _____ are an example of violent herd mentality. For instance, ❺ _____ celebrating a sports victory may burn cars and ❻ _____ buildings. Following ❼ _____ is a nonviolent example. On Black Friday in the United States, ❽ _____ lose their minds by ❾ _____ as much as they can. Some people engage in herd mentality to feel safe while others just lose ❿ _____ while in a crowd.

Unit 4 **Amnesia**

Vocabulary

A **Read the sentences and choose the best words for the blanks.**

1 His **permanent** brain damage is likely to last _____.

a. forever   b. a while   c. until tomorrow   d. a year

2 She suffered a **traumatic** injury which is still extremely _____ for her.

a. painful   b. funny   c. expensive   d. old

3 Joe is trying to **regain** his stolen possessions because he wants to get them _____.

a. away   b. over   c. back   d. under

B **Choose the words from the box to complete the sentences.**

last	adjust	condition	sufferers	previous

1 This medical _____ will likely continue around a month.

2 His recovery is expected to _____ around four or five weeks.

3 Some _____ of the disease are able to recover completely.

4 The doctors think the patient can _____ to her new condition soon.

5 On her _____ trip to the hospital, the doctor gave her some medicine.

Translation

C **Read the sentences and translate them into your language.**

1 The event is very severe, so the sufferer has no memory of it.

→ _____

2 Nor can they recall the activities they did the previous day.

→ _____

3 A person who is unable to remember events before a certain date has the former.

→ _____

Paraphrasing

D **Paraphrase the sentences from the passage with the phrases in the box.**

a car crash	get used to	happens to people
had forgotten	head problems	an upsetting event

1 Still, over time, most people remember what they once could not.

→ Still, most people usually remember what they _____ .

2 A person with this type of amnesia often has difficulty adjusting to life.

→ This kind of amnesia is hard for people to _____ life.

3 Known as amnesia, this condition tends to occur when people have head injuries or catch certain diseases.

→ Amnesia often _____ due to _____ or certain illnesses.

4 This may happen to a person when a traumatic event such as a violent attack or a car accident takes place.

→ _____ like a violent attack or _____ may cause this.

Listening

E **Listen to the summary and fill in the blanks.**

People may ❶ _____ from memory ❷ _____ after getting a head injury or a disease. People with ❸ _____ usually get one of two main types. Retrograde amnesia occurs when a person cannot ❹ _____ events before a certain date. However, people with it can ❺ _____ new memories. People with anterograde amnesia can remember the ❻ _____ but cannot form new ❼ _____ . These individuals usually have difficulty ❽ _____ to life. Amnesia can be permanent or ❾ _____ . Most sufferers recover quickly. But those experiencing ❿ _____ events such as car accidents or violent attacks may get permanent amnesia.

Unit 5 The Search for El Dorado

Vocabulary

A **Read the sentences and choose the best words for the blanks.**

1 The new **chief** is an excellent _____ of his tribe.

    a. member   b. leader   c. ancestor   d. follower

2 They are in danger of dying of **starvation** since they lack _____.

    a. money   b. shelter   c. warmth   d. food

3 The general **conquered** the enemy army by _____ it in battle.

    a. losing to   b. fighting   c. defeating   d. challenging

B **Choose the words from the box to complete the sentences.**

myths	execute	explorer	supposedly	convince

1 He was a great _____ who discovered some new lands.

2 There are many _____ about lost cities around the world.

3 She tried to _____ him that the treasure did not exist.

4 It was _____ a city that had been built in the jungle.

5 The leader will _____ the men who stole the gold from the tribe.

Translation

C **Read the sentences and translate them into your language.**

1 Whenever a new chief rose to power, there was a special ceremony.

   ➡ _____

2 Instead of a man covered in gold, there was a city made of gold called El Dorado.

   ➡ _____

3 They claim it is hidden by the jungle and is waiting for some brave explorers to find it.

   ➡ _____

Paraphrasing

D **Paraphrase the sentences from the passage with the words and phrases in the box.**

hunger	the legend	be built	lots of adventurers
died because of	believed the story	find gold	to begin

1 Supposedly a city made entirely of gold, it was searched for by many explorers.

→ _____ searched for a city said to _____ of gold.

2 Yet the story convinced many explorers, greedy for gold, to travel to the New World.

→ Many explorers _____, so they went to the Americas to _____.

3 Explorers and their men were often killed by disease, starvation, and natives.

→ Explorers and their men _____ illness, _____, and natives.

4 The myth of El Dorado arose due to a custom by the Muisca people of Colombia.

→ A tradition of the Muisca people caused _____ of El Dorado _____.

Listening

E **Listen to the summary and fill in the blanks.**

The Spanish ❶ _____ for gold in South America in the 1500s and 1600s. There was a ❷ _____ by the Muisca people of Colombia. They ❸ _____ their new chief in gold ❹ _____ and called him *el dorado*, meaning "one covered in gold." But the story ❺ _____ to a city ❻ _____ of gold. The Spanish and other ❼ _____ such as Sir Walter Raleigh tried to find El Dorado. Their ❽ _____ were all ❾ _____, and many men died. Most people quit searching for El Dorado in the late 1600s, but some people still believe it ❿ _____.

Unit 6 All Roads Lead to Rome

Vocabulary

A **Read the sentences and choose the best words for the blanks.**

1 The **decorative** ornaments made the room look very _____.

a. untidy   b. pretty   c. straight   d. small

2 There were too many **obstacles** _____ the road while we were driving.

a. running on   b. destroying   c. crossing   d. blocking

3 It is necessary to **drain** the water to _____ it from the basement.

a. remove   b. fill   c. add   d. clean

B **Choose the words from the box to complete the sentences.**

extensive	capital	outstanding	trench	possesses

1 The _____ of the empire is the largest city in the area.

2 They dug a deep _____ for water to pass through.

3 The engineer is _____, so he can build strong bridges.

4 Thanks to the _____ number of roads, transportation there is easy.

5 The empire _____ many lands that it conquered during wars.

Translation

C **Read the sentences and translate them into your language.**

1 The Romans, who were outstanding engineers, developed an extensive road system.

→ _____

2 First, they dug trenches and filled them with sand or dirt.

→ _____

3 Most importantly, the roads were built so that they eventually led to Rome.

→ _____

Paraphrasing

D **Paraphrase the sentences from the passage with the phrases in the box.**

like turns	sailed on ships	hundreds of years ago
the expression	straight roads	to anywhere else

1 The origins of this idiom go back centuries to the Roman Empire.

→ _____ started in the Roman Empire _____.

2 People could travel to some parts of the empire by ship, but they mostly traveled on land.

→ Some people _____, but most traveled around the empire on land.

3 The Romans preferred to avoid turns, so they built roads straight through natural obstacles.

→ The Romans did not _____, so they made _____ through natural obstacles.

4 This allowed the Romans to travel from their capital to anywhere in the empire as directly as possible.

→ The Romans were able to go from the capital directly _____ in the empire.

Listening

E **Listen to the summary and fill in the blanks.**

The ❶ _____ "All roads lead to Rome" was based on the fact that all roads in the Roman Empire ❷ _____ went to Rome. The Romans had an ❸ _____ road system with more than 400,000 kilometers of roads. The Romans ❹ _____ straight roads, so they ❺ _____ their roads through natural ❻ _____. They made roads with large and small rocks, ❼ _____, and basalt. The roads were wide enough for foot ❽ _____ and ❾ _____ vehicles. They were so well made that some of them ❿ _____ today.

Unit 7 **Science Fiction**

Vocabulary

A **Read the sentences and choose the best words for the blanks.**

1 The **genre** of science fiction is the _____ of writing that he likes the most.

    a. period   b. type   c. part   d. story

2 The explorers had many _____ while they were on their **adventure**.

    a. experiences   b. countries   c. topics   d. superheroes

3 The company will **publish** the book and _____ more than 10,000 copies of it.

    a. write   b. advertise   c. print   d. order

B **Choose the words from the box to complete the sentences.**

superheroes	progressing	aliens	political	invasion

1 The work has been _____ well.

2 He has some _____ experience, so he will run for president.

3 He does not believe _____ exist even though he has seen a UFO.

4 Batman and Wonder Woman are two popular _____ in comic books.

5 In the story, an alien _____ was responsible for the destruction of the Earth.

Translation

C **Read the sentences and translate them into your language.**

1 As science-fiction writing progressed, it began looking to the stars.

  → _____

2 Lots of science-fiction stories are about science and technology, aliens, and other worlds.

  → _____

3 While he is successful, the monster he creates destroys not only that man but also the people he loves.

  → _____

Paraphrasing

D **Paraphrase the sentences from the passage with the phrases in the box.**

> great novel   stressed the threats   many people
> became popular   the early years   superhero films   the appeal

1 The twentieth century saw the popularity of science fiction increase greatly.

→ Science fiction _____ with many people in the 1900s.

2 In 1818, Mary Shelley published *Frankenstein*, one of the greatest works in English literature.

→ Mary Shelley wrote the _____ *Frankenstein* in 1818.

3 The first few decades of science fiction focused on science and technology and the dangers they posed.

→ _____ of science fiction _____ of science and technology.

4 In more recent times, *Iron Man*, *The Avengers*, and other superhero movies have made science fiction more popular than ever before.

→ Lately, various _____ have increased _____ of science fiction to _____.

Listening

E **Listen to the summary and fill in the blanks.**

> Mary Shelley ❶ _____ *Frankenstein* in 1818 and wrote the first real work of
> science fiction. This is a genre of ❷ _____ fiction that ❸ _____
> on science and technology, aliens, and other worlds. Writers like Shelley and Robert Louis
> Stevenson, who ❹ _____ *Strange Case of Dr. Jekyll and Mr. Hyde*, wrote about the
> ❺ _____ of science and technology. Later writers, such as Jules Verne and H.G.
> Wells, wrote about the stars and alien ❻ _____. In the ❼ _____
> century, writers put ❽ _____ and environmental topics into their ❾ _____.
> Many science-fiction stories were made into ❿ _____, which helped science fiction
> become more popular.

Unit 8 Famous Detectives in Literature

Vocabulary

A **Read the sentences and choose the best words for the blanks.**

1 The story **features** a villain, who has a major _____ in the tale.

    a. problem   b. part   c. story   d. side

2 She is a famous **novelist** whose works of _____ sell millions of copies.

    a. fiction   b. research   c. poems   d. nonfiction

3 When he _____ the person in the story, most readers were shocked by the **murder**.

    a. introduced   b. laughed at   c. killed   d. fired

B **Choose the words from the box to complete the sentences.**

case	evidence	crimes	intuition	villain

1 The number of violent _____ has increased recently.

2 The detective is looking for _____ in order to solve the crime.

3 In the story, the _____ steals some gold and tries to escape with it.

4 Some people use their feelings and _____ to determine what is correct.

5 The police have been trying to solve the murder _____ for months.

Translation

C **Read the sentences and translate them into your language.**

1 He can solve cases just by getting people to talk to him.

    → _____

2 He also notices small bits of evidence and uses them to figure out the problem.

    → _____

3 Holmes is a highly intelligent man who uses logic to solve mysteries.

    → _____

Paraphrasing

D **Paraphrase the sentences from the passage with the phrases in the box.**

how criminals think	responsible for	bestselling writer
not long	figures out cases	their own detectives

1 Poe is widely credited for inventing the detective genre.

→ People say that Poe was _____ inventing the detective genre.

2 Hercule Poirot is the creation of Agatha Christie, one of the bestselling novelists ever.

→ _____ Agatha Christie made Hercule Poirot.

3 To solve the cases, Dupin uses his intelligence and reasoning to get inside the minds of criminals.

→ Dupin _____ by using intelligence and logic to understand _____ .

4 Dupin inspired many other detectives that authors wrote about soon afterward.

→ _____ afterward, other writers were inspired by Dupin to create _____ .

Listening

E **Listen to the summary and fill in the blanks.**

The detective ❶ _____ involves a person trying to ❷ _____ a crime. It was ❸ _____ by Edgar Allan Poe, who wrote "The Murders in the Rue Morgue," which ❹ _____ C. Auguste Dupin. Dupin uses ❺ _____ and ❻ _____ to solve crimes. Sir Arthur Conan Doyle ❼ _____ Sherlock Holmes on Dupin. Holmes is very intelligent and solves crimes by using small bits of ❽ _____ . Agatha Christie put Hercule Poirot into more than thirty novels and fifty short stories. He uses ❾ _____ but can also solve cases with ❿ _____ and feelings.

Unit 9 **Rediscovered Species**

Vocabulary

A **Read the sentences and choose the best words for the blanks.**

1 The **diets** of most animals include _____ that they find or hunt.

   a. herds   b. leaves   c. water   d. food

2 When the Romans **ruled** in Europe, they _____ most of the land there.

   a. controlled   b. bought   c. farmed   d. lived on

3 These **tiny** animals are so _____ that you cannot see them without a microscope.

   a. interesting   b. small   c. dangerous   d. unimportant

B **Choose the words from the box to complete the sentences.**

prehistoric	extinct	colonies	billions	exploring

1 Some ant _____ may have millions of insects living in them.

2 The dodo bird went _____ because it could not defend itself.

3 During _____ times, humans mostly lived primitive lives.

4 They are _____ the jungle to try to find some new animal species.

5 Experts believe that there has been life on the Earth for _____ of years.

Translation

C **Read the sentences and translate them into your language.**

1 It was a prehistoric fish that lived millions of years ago.

  → _____

2 In 1938, a living coelacanth was found off the coast of South Africa.

  → _____

3 Yet at least one animal that lived during the time of the dinosaurs is a rediscovered species.

  → _____

Paraphrasing

D **Paraphrase the sentences from the passage with the words and phrases in the box.**

any dinosaurs	went extinct	adventuring	probably
has been	be extinct	people believed	nobody

1 Scientists believe that life has existed on the Earth for at least 3.8 billion years.

→ Scientists think life _____ on the Earth for billions of years.

2 Another animal, the Laotian rock rat, was thought to have gone extinct ten million years ago.

→ _____ the Laotian rock rat _____ ten million years ago.

3 The dinosaurs are not rediscovered species since nobody has found any alive today.

→ _____ has found _____ alive today, so they are not rediscovered species.

4 As people explore more places around the world, they will likely find even more animals once thought to be dead.

→ When _____ around the world, people will _____ find more animals thought to _____.

Listening

E **Listen to the summary and fill in the blanks.**

Species have been going ❶ _____ for the past 3.8 billion years. But sometimes animals thought to be extinct are ❷ _____ alive. These are ❸ _____ species. One, the coelacanth, was found in 1938 after people thought it had ❹ _____ ❺ _____ sixty-five million years ago. People also believed the gracilidris, a ❻ _____ ant, and the Laotian rock rat had ❼ _____ extinct. But they were found in South America and Laos, respectively. Some rediscovered species are ❽ _____ to have died ❾ _____ of years ago while others are believed to have ❿ _____ a short time ago.

Unit 10 Beavers: Keystone Species

Vocabulary

A **Read the sentences and choose the best words for the blanks.**

1 Blue jays are **thriving** in this area and are quite a _____ species.

   a. noisy   b. social   c. successful   d. endangered

2 The ecosystem **collapsed** and totally _____ when the keystone species died.

   a. changed   b. got better   c. fell apart   d. appeared

3 The river **eroded** the land and _____ the soil in the area it flowed through.

   a. broke down   b. built up   c. strengthened   d. gave nutrients to

B **Choose the words from the box to complete the sentences.**

pests	pollutants	swampy	ecosystem	breeding grounds

1 The ocean _____ has all kinds of life in it.

2 The _____ in the air are making it hard to breathe.

3 Many kinds of animals use _____ areas to lay eggs.

4 Farmers use various methods to kill _____ in their fields.

5 Some whales travel thousands of kilometers to reach their _____.

Translation

C **Read the sentences and translate them into your language.**

1 In fact, if a keystone species disappeared, its ecosystem would collapse.

   → _____

2 When beavers dam flowing water, they create new ecosystems.

   → _____

3 When various pollutants reach the dams, they get stopped and then cannot head downstream.

   → _____

Paraphrasing

D **Paraphrase the sentences from the passage with the words and phrases in the box.**

reside	create	halt or lessen	live in water
understand	useful animals	make dams	various animals

1 Biologists have realized that rather than being pests, beavers are actually quite helpful.

→ Biologists now _____ that beavers are very _____ , not pests.

2 Countless fish, birds, mammals, and other animals live in the wetlands beavers make.

→ _____ _____ in the wetlands that beavers _____ .

3 When there are heavy rains, the dams can stop floods from occurring or reduce their effects.

→ The dams _____ the effects of floods during heavy rains.

4 Beavers are semiaquatic mammals known mostly for building dams across streams, creeks, and rivers.

→ People know beavers as mammals that mostly _____ and that _____ .

Listening

E **Listen to the summary and fill in the blanks.**

People used to kill beavers because of the dams they ❶ _____ across streams and rivers. However, beavers are making a ❷ _____ because scientists now know they are ❸ _____ species. These are animals that are ❹ _____ to their ❺ _____ . Beaver dams create new ecosystems that many kinds of animals live in. Some are even ❻ _____ species. They use the areas around the dams as ❼ _____ grounds. In addition, beaver dams prevent erosion and stop ❽ _____ . They also remove ❾ _____ from water. For these reasons, people have started ❿ _____ beavers to areas.

Unit 11 Memorable Commercials

Vocabulary

A **Read the sentences and choose the best words for the blanks.**

1 The machine is very **effective** when it is working _____.

    a. slowly   b. suddenly   c. finally   d. properly

2 Mary **complimented** John and said something _____ about him.

    a. bad   b. silly   c. strange   d. nice

3 As a **marketer**, Eric tries to _____ his company's products to people.

    a. give   b. sell   c. purchase   d. build

B **Choose the words from the box to complete the sentences.**

commercial	visual	responded	memorable	slogan

1 _____ images can be very powerful for a lot of young shoppers.

2 People remember some _____ ads decades after they were made.

3 They _____ positively to the attempts to get them to buy the product.

4 The company decided to advertise its products with a TV _____.

5 The company needs to have a _____ so that people will remember the phrase.

Translation

C **Read the sentences and translate them into your language.**

1 While people remember funny ads, they often forget the products.

   ➔ _____

2 Using icons is another way to make effective commercials.

   ➔ _____

3 The 1984 ad would become one of the most memorable commercials in history.

   ➔ _____

Paraphrasing

D **Paraphrase the sentences from the passage with the words and phrases in the box.**

buy	does not stop	memorable ads
other batteries	appeared	do not use	millions of people

1 The woman was Clara Peller, and she was in an ad for the fast-food chain Wendy's.

→ Clara Peller _____ in a commercial for a fast-food restaurant.

2 Marketers who want to create ads that people remember frequently avoid humor.

→ Marketers often _____ humor to create _____.

3 This toy rabbit, which is powered by Energizer batteries, keeps going when other toys using different batteries have stopped.

→ The toy rabbit, which uses Energizer batteries, _____ while toys with _____ do.

4 Nike used that slogan to sell millions of the Air Jordan basketball sneakers worn by Michael Jordan in the 1980s and 1990s.

→ Nike had a slogan it used to get _____ to _____ Michael Jordan's shoes in the past.

Listening

E **Listen to the summary and fill in the blanks.**

In a famous Wendy's ❶ _____, Clara Peller looks at a small hamburger and asks, "Where's the beef?" This ad is one of the most ❷ _____ in history. Marketers often use ❸ _____ to create memorable ads. "Just do it" is a Nike tagline, and "Have a Coke and a smile" is a tagline in ❹ _____ commercials for Coca-Cola. ❺ _____ such as the Energizer Bunny can make ❻ _____ commercials. ❼ _____ can use ❽ _____ humor in their ads. But people often forget the products being ❾ _____ in funny ads, so marketers often ❿ _____ using humor.

Unit 12 **Marketing through Social Media**

Vocabulary

A   **Read the sentences and choose the best words for the blanks.**

1 The **link** between the two companies is a very strong _____.

   a. contract   b. connection   c. proposal   d. period

2 Most businesspeople **interact** by communicating _____ with one another.

   a. rarely   b. particularly   c. directly   d. pleasantly

3 When her video **went viral**, it became extremely _____ around the world.

   a. popular   b. obvious   c. rare   d. disliked

B   **Choose the words from the box to complete the sentences.**

customer base	updates	profit	promote	posts

1 It is important for companies to provide their _____ regularly.

2 The _____ of that firm is growing due to the quality of its products.

3 He intends to _____ the new service on TV as well as on the Internet.

4 The company often _____ information about its new products on its website.

5 The business made a huge _____ thanks to the success of its commercials.

Translation

C   **Read the sentences and translate them into your language.**

1 They let their friends and family members see what they are doing.

   → _____

2 But a restaurant that serves food people do not like may get complaints.

   → _____

3 A travel agency that posts pictures of the tours it leads may get positive comments from customers.

   → _____

Paraphrasing

D **Paraphrase the sentences from the passage with the phrases in the box.**

post it	buy from them	be viewed
new material	what is happening	get closer

1 People use these websites and others to provide updates on their personal lives.

→ These webpages let others know _____ in people's personal lives.

2 Businesses use SMM by creating content and by sharing it on social media.

→ Businesses make _____ and _____ on SMM.

3 One benefit of SMM is that it brings businesses closer to their customers.

→ SMM helps businesses _____ to the people who _____.

4 Thousands or millions of people may view a post on Facebook or a tweet on Twitter that goes viral.

→ Posts or tweets that go viral may _____ by thousands or millions of people.

Listening

E **Listen to the summary and fill in the blanks.**

Nowadays, hundreds of ❶ _____ of people use a variety of social media websites. ❷ _____ are using them as well. Businesses ❸ _____ their products by creating a variety of ❹ _____ and posting it online. This is called social media marketing (SMM). One ❺ _____ of SMM is that it brings businesses and their customers ❻ _____. Customers can ❼ _____ with businesses and make positive or ❽ _____ comments. These can help businesses ❾ _____ the quality of their service. SMM can also help people learn about a business, especially if an SMM post goes ❿ _____.

Unit 13 Medieval Wandering Minstrels

Vocabulary

A **Read the sentences and choose the best words for the blanks.**

1 Medieval **peasants** were poor _____ who rented land from a noble.

   a. soldiers   b. tradesmen   c. students   d. farmers

2 If you **memorize** the answers, you will _____ them during the test.

   a. remember   b. correct   c. forget   d. mistake

3 **Wandering** minstrels were always busy _____ one place to another.

   a. working in   b. studying   c. traveling from   d. staying in

B **Choose the words from the box to complete the sentences.**

medieval	recited	entertained	juggler	feast

1 Wandering minstrels _____ people with stories and songs.

2 The poet _____ the work he had written to the audience.

3 At the _____, the people enjoyed many different kinds of food.

4 During _____ times, most people farmed the land every day.

5 People enjoyed watching the _____ keep ten balls in the air for a while.

Translation

C **Read the sentences and translate them into your language.**

1 In Europe during the Middle Ages, there were few forms of entertainment.

   → _____

2 These allowed peasants to take a break from working and to enjoy themselves.

   → _____

3 Since they traveled from town to town to perform, minstrels carried light instruments.

   → _____

Paraphrasing

D **Paraphrase the sentences from the passage with the words and phrases in the box.**

	focused on	attended	traveled to
	well regarded	gathered news	regular performers

1 Minstrels were entertainers who were common from the 1100s to the 1600s.

→ Minstrels were _____ for around 500 years.

2 Many of their songs and tales had to do with chivalry and courtly love.

→ Their songs and stories _____ chivalry and courtly love.

3 As minstrels often moved, they collected news in the many towns they visited.

→ Minstrels _____ in the places they _____ .

4 Among the most popular people at these special events were wandering minstrels.

→ Wandering minstrels who _____ these events were _____ .

Listening

E **Listen to the summary and fill in the blanks.**

❶ _____ in the Middle Ages had hard lives and few forms of ❷ _____ .
There were some special events, and ❸ _____ minstrels were among the most
popular people who ❹ _____ them. Minstrels were not just singers but were also
❺ _____ and acrobats. They told ❻ _____ , did magic tricks, and put
on animal shows. They carried light ❼ _____ . They sang ❽ _____
and ballads, and they often sang about chivalry and ❾ _____ love. Minstrels also
❿ _____ news, so they told people in other towns the news they had learned
elsewhere.

Unit 14 Glass Art

Vocabulary

A **Read the sentences and choose the best words for the blanks.**

1 Please use your **imagination** to _____ some new ideas.

   a. sell   b. discuss   c. think of   d. draw

2 At the **dig site**, the archaeologists found many objects in the _____.

   a. museum   b. building   c. ground   d. collection

3 We need some **practical** ideas that are _____ to lots of people.

   a. useful   b. hopeful   c. fascinating   d. clear

B **Choose the words from the box to complete the sentences.**

beads	cathedral	statue	prominent	assemble

1 Tools are needed to _____ this furniture.

2 The painting has a _____ position in the museum.

3 There are many stained-glass windows in the _____.

4 The necklace is made of a large number of small glass _____.

5 There is a large _____ of a bull at the front of the museum.

Translation

C **Read the sentences and translate them into your language.**

1 These windows were so well made that, centuries later, they still exist in many structures.

  → _____

2 Archaeologists have dug up glass beads at many dig sites around the world.

  → _____

3 They blow glass into different shapes and then assemble them into works resembling statues.

  → _____

Paraphrasing

D **Paraphrase the sentences from the passage with the words and phrases in the box.**

making	use a method	was developed	an additional type
requires the use	any kind of art	creating art	think of

1 The artwork created with this method is limited only by the artist's imagination.

→ Artists can use this method to make _____ that they can _____.

2 People have been making glass art almost since the art of glassblowing was invented.

→ Since glassblowing _____, people have been _____ with glass.

3 Some artists like to take thick pieces of glass and then use a procedure called sandblasting.

→ Artists _____ called sandblasting that _____ of thick glass.

4 Another form of glass art was blowing glass into shapes such as vases and pots.

→ _____ of glass art was _____ vases and pots by blowing glass.

Listening

E **Listen to the summary and fill in the blanks.**

Since people ❶ _____ the art of ❷ _____, they have been making glass art. Some people made glass beads as ❸ _____ while others blew glass into ❹ _____ and pots that they then decorated. ❺ _____ windows are the best-known type of glass art. They were found in churches and ❻ _____ in Europe in the Middle Ages. They featured ❼ _____ from the Bible. In modern times, some artists create glass ❽ _____. Others use sandblasting to remove parts of the ❾ _____ of glass to create sculptures. Others cut glass with diamond ❿ _____ and lasers to make glass art.

Unit 15 **Tropical Cyclones**

Vocabulary

A **Read the sentences and choose the best words for the blanks.**

1 The storm moved **inland** and went _____ the ocean.

a. away from   b. close to   c. over   d. beside

2 The **violent** storm had so much _____ that it destroyed many homes.

a. anger   b. power   c. rain   d. size

3 The river level _____, so there was some **flooding** in the city last night.

a. moved   b. rose   c. lowered   d. sank

B **Choose the words from the box to complete the sentences.**

equator	made landfall	condense	destruction	swirl

1 One of the most violent storms _____ in the city yesterday.

2 Water vapor can _____ and form tiny droplets of water in the air.

3 The winds began to _____ around until a cyclone suddenly formed.

4 The closer to the _____ a person is, the hotter the weather becomes.

5 The snowstorm was so heavy that it caused the _____ of some buildings.

Translation

C **Read the sentences and translate them into your language.**

1 The constant spinning and the forming of clouds create a storm.

→ _____

2 The warm ocean water heats the air, which gets pushed upward.

→ _____

3 For this reason, tropical cyclones form in waters relatively close to the equator.

→ _____

Paraphrasing

D **Paraphrase the sentences from the passage with the phrases in the box.**

makes floods	is made	a lot of damage	starts circling faster
takes place	certain conditions	move over land	to be created

1 As the storm rotates faster, an eye forms in its center.

→ An eye _____ in the center when the storm _____.

2 For a tropical cyclone to form, the proper environmental conditions must exist.

→ _____ must exist for a tropical cyclone _____.

3 When tropical cyclones make landfall, they can cause tremendous amounts of destruction.

→ Tropical cyclones cause _____ when they _____.

4 That usually happens after the rain has caused flooding and the high winds have caused great damage.

→ That usually _____ once rain _____ and winds cause a lot of damage.

Listening

E **Listen to the summary and fill in the blanks.**

Tropical cyclones are violent storms that ❶ _____ in warm water near the ❷ _____. When air gets ❸ _____, it rises and forms a low-pressure ❹ _____. Air from high-pressure zones moves in, where it gets warm and ❺ _____ and then rises. The air ❻ _____, and clouds form, creating a storm. When the storm's winds ❼ _____ fast enough, it becomes a tropical cyclone. The storm moves across the ocean and gains ❽ _____ by taking in water from the ocean below. When it goes onto land, it rains ❾ _____ and causes ❿ _____ and flooding.

Unit 16 How Ice Ages Occur

Vocabulary

A **Read the sentences and choose the best words for the blanks.**

1 The amount of ice **declined** and _____ very quickly.

   a. froze   b. expanded   c. appeared   d. went down

2 If you _____ anything, see if you can **identify** it.

   a. recognize   b. get   c. lose   d. mention

3 The water **cycle** is something that _____ constantly.

   a. exists   b. changes   c. moves   d. repeats

B **Choose the words from the box to complete the sentences.**

major	orbit	polar caps	undergo	greenhouse gases

1 The Earth's _____ takes a bit more than 365 days to conclude.

2 A(n) _____ ice age took place on the Earth for millions of years.

3 The weather may _____ serious changes from winter to summer.

4 Carbon dioxide is one of the best-known of all the _____.

5 The _____ get bigger and smaller depending on the temperature.

Translation

C **Read the sentences and translate them into your language.**

1 There is sometimes so little energy that the planet enters an ice age.

  → _____

2 Throughout Earth's existence, there have been five major ice ages.

  → _____

3 When there are few greenhouse gases such as carbon dioxide, the planet can cool.

  → _____

Paraphrasing

D **Paraphrase the sentences from the passage with the phrases in the box.**

	a lack of	gets very cold	distant from	
goes down	still happening	moves outward	temperature drop	

1 When the Earth's orbit is farther from the sun, the temperature becomes much colder.

→ When the Earth is _____ the sun, the temperature _____.

2 When there are few volcanic eruptions, the Earth's temperature can decline.

→ _____ volcanoes erupting can make the Earth's _____.

3 The Earth endures periods of extreme cold, and the ice at its polar caps expands greatly.

→ When the Earth _____, ice from the polar caps _____.

4 The shortest ice age, called the Quaternary Ice Age, started 2.5 million years ago and is still going on.

→ The Quaternary Ice Age started millions of years ago and is _____.

Listening

E **Listen to the summary and fill in the blanks.**

The Earth's ❶ _____ constantly undergoes changes, and ice ❷ _____ sometimes happen. There have been five major ice ages. The Quaternary Ice Age is the ❸ _____ one and is still going on. The Earth is now in an ❹ _____ period, so it is warm between very cold ❺ _____. Ice ages happen for many ❻ _____. The sun might produce less ❼ _____, or the Earth might ❽ _____ far from the sun. The planet can cool when there are few ❾ _____ gases in the atmosphere, too. That can happen when there are few volcanic ❿ _____.

Remember

Further
Writing Practice

Unit 1 **Ancient Food Preservation Methods**

Q Do you know how to preserve any kind of food? What steps are required?

A The following table shows some ideas for answering the question above. Check the one that you like the most. If you have your own idea, write it in the last row.

Kind of Food	Steps
☐ strawberry jam	• Cut the strawberries into even pieces. Then, mash them and add sugar. • Boil the mixture for 20 minutes and wait a few minutes for it to cool. Then, transfer it to a clean jar and put it in the refrigerator.
☐ pickles	• Add spices and vinegar to water and then boil it for a few minutes. • Pour the mixture into jars and then put cucumbers in them. Seal the jars and then put them in the refrigerator.
☐ dried fruit	• Cut the fruit into thin slices and then place it onto trays. Be sure the pieces do not touch one another. • Put the trays outside on a hot, sunny day. Keep the trays out in the sun for several days until they are fully dried.

B Read the question again and complete the following paragraph.

I know how to preserve a few kinds of food. One kind of food I would like to preserve is

_____. It is really easy to do. First, _____

_____.

After that, _____

_____.

Unit 2 Lost Tribes of the Amazon

Q **What is a tribe that has not made contact with modern people? Where does the tribe live, and what are the tribe members' lives like?**

A The following table shows some ideas for answering the question above. Check the one that you like the most. If you have your own idea, write it in the last row.

Tribe	Characteristics
☐ Sentinelese	• They live on North Sentinel Island between India and Thailand. • They have been uncontacted for thousands of years, and they hunt and fish for food. They are hostile to outsiders, so they attack people who land on their island.
☐ Korubo	• They live in the Amazon Rainforest near the border of Brazil and Peru. • They survive by hunting and gathering food in the rainforest. They carry big clubs to defend themselves with.
☐ Yaifo	• They live in the jungles of Papua New Guinea, an island near Australia. • They use bows and arrows for hunting and are believed to be headhunters. So they cut off the heads of their enemies and preserve them.

B Read the question again and complete the following paragraph.

One tribe that has not made contact with modern people is the _____.

They live _____.

As for their lives, they _____

_____

_____.

Unit 3 Mob Mentality

Q   **What is an historical example of mob mentality? What happened that made people act in this manner?**

A   The following table shows some ideas for answering the question above. Check the one that you like the most. If you have your own idea, write it in the last row.

Event	Actions
☐ the Dot-Com Bubble	• People were excited about the Internet, so they began investing millions of dollars in Internet startups. • The bubble burst, so the stock prices of many Internet startups dropped rapidly, and lots of them went out of business.
☐ the French Revolution	• People across France rebelled against the king and made demands for democracy. • The revolution got out of control, and thousands of people were executed by having their heads chopped off.
☐ the Salem Witch Trials	• Some girls acted strangely and claimed that witches were affecting their behavior. • People in Salem accused many others of being witches, so more than 200 people were accused, and twenty were killed.

B   Read the question again and complete the following paragraph.

One historical example of mob mentality is _____. It started when _____

_____.

After that, _____

_____

_____.

Unit 4 **Amnesia**

Q
What is a common mental problem or illness that people suffer from? What are some characteristics of it?

A
The following table shows some ideas for answering the question above. Check the one that you like the most. If you have your own idea, write it in the last row.

Mental Problem/Illness	Characteristics
☐ dementia	• People begin to lose their ability to think as they age. • Their understanding, thoughts, memories, and language skills slowly get worse over time.
☐ anxiety	• People worry too much about things, especially those that are not particularly important. • They may be nervous, have trouble concentrating, be irritable, and feel tense.
☐ depression	• People are affected by strong feelings of sadness. • They may lose interest in doing various activities, have trouble sleeping, and feel exhausted all the time.

B
Read the question again and complete the following paragraph.

One common mental illness is _____. People with it _____
_____.
They / Their _____
_____
_____.

Unit 5 The Search for El Dorado

Q **What is a lost city or land that you know about? Where was it, and why did it become lost?**

A The following table shows some ideas for answering the question above. Check the one that you like the most. If you have your own idea, write it in the last row.

Lost City/Land	Location and Characteristics
☐ Atlantis	• It may have been in the Mediterranean Sea or in the Atlantic Ocean. • It was an island that suddenly sank into the water and completely disappeared.
☐ Avalon	• It was an island located somewhere in Great Britain. • King Arthur was taken there to recover from his injuries in a battle. The island was then hidden in mist until King Arthur returns someday.
☐ Agartha	• It is a kingdom that is located inside the Earth near the core. • The people there are wise and wealthy, and they live hidden until humans are one day good enough to meet them.

B Read the question again and complete the following paragraph.

One lost land that I know about is _____. It is said to be located _____
_____.

It is believed that _____
_____
_____.

Unit 6 All Roads Lead to Rome

Q **What is a famous road you know about? Where is it, and what makes it so famous?**

A The following table shows some ideas for answering the question above. Check the one that you like the most. If you have your own idea, write it in the last row.

Road	Location and Features
☐ Route 66	• It went from Chicago, Illinois, to Los Angeles, California. • Many people traveling west in the United States drove on it. It became a famous symbol of the United States.
☐ the Champs-Elysées	• It is a wide avenue that runs through a part of Paris, France. • The road ends at the Arc de Triomphe, which celebrated the victories of Napoleon Bonaparte. Cyclists in the Tour de France ride down it on the last day of the race.
☐ Orchard Road	• It runs through the shopping district in Singapore. • Many expensive stores line the street, making it popular with shoppers. The residence of the president of Singapore is also found on this road.

B Read the question again and complete the following paragraph.

One famous road I know is _____ . It _____

_____ .

It is so famous because _____

_____

_____ .

Unit 7 Science Fiction

Q **What is a popular genre of literature that you enjoy reading? What are some features of that genre, and what are some books in it?**

A The following table shows some ideas for answering the question above. Check the one that you like the most. If you have your own idea, write it in the last row.

Genre	Features and Books
☐ fantasy	• It often features magic or supernatural events and characters. • *The Lord of the Rings* by J.R.R. Tolkien and the *Harry Potter* books by J.K. Rowling are works of fantasy.
☐ horror	• It is meant to scare the people who read them. • *Dracula* by Bram Stoker and *The Call of Cthulhu* by H.P. Lovecraft are two works of horror.
☐ historical fiction	• It tells a story that is based in a historical time period and has people who really lived and events that actually happened in it. • Two works of historical fiction are *The Last of the Mohicans* by James Fenimore Cooper and *The Three Musketeers* by Alexander Dumas.

B Read the question again and complete the following paragraph.

I enjoy reading _____. One feature of this genre is that _____
_____.

Some well-known works in this genre are _____
_____.

Unit 8 Famous Detectives in Literature

Q Who is your favorite fictional detective? What methods does the detective use to solve cases?

A The following table shows some ideas for answering the question above. Check the one that you like the most. If you have your own idea, write it in the last row.

Fictional Detective	Methods
☐ Encyclopedia Brown	• He listens to his father, a policeman, tell him about some problems and then asks questions about the cases. • He uses his great intelligence to determine who the villain in the story is.
☐ Nancy Drew	• She is a teenager who often helps her father, a lawyer, solve some of his cases. • She uses her intelligence and knowledge of psychology to understand how and why people behave.
☐ Mike Hammer	• He is a private detective who is hired by people to solve mysteries, often murders. • He uses violence and often fights people when he tries to solve cases.

B Read the question again and complete the following paragraph.

My favorite fictional detective is _____. He/She _____

_____.

He/She often solves cases by _____

_____.

Unit 9 Rediscovered Species

Q   **What is an animal you know that has gone extinct? What was it, and what made it become extinct?**

A   The following table shows some ideas for answering the question above. Check the one that you like the most. If you have your own idea, write it in the last row.

Extinct Species	When and Why It Disappeared
☐ dodo bird	• It was a flightless bird that lived on Mauritius, an island located in the Indian Ocean. • It had no natural predators until humans arrived. Then, humans and animals such as dogs and cats hunted it until it died out in 1662.
☐ megalodon	• It was an enormous shark that could be nearly twenty meters in length. • It went extinct around 3.6 million years ago and may have died out because its food supply was affected.
☐ auroch	• It was a huge type of cow with long horns that used to live in many parts of Europe. • It went extinct in 1627. People hunted it and destroyed its habitat because of farming.

B   Read the question again and complete the following paragraph.

One animal that is no longer alive is _____. It was _____.

It _____

_____.

44

Unit 10 Beavers: Keystone Species

Q   **What is a keystone species that you know about? What makes it a keystone species?**

A   The following table shows some ideas for answering the question above. Check the one that you like the most. If you have your own idea, write it in the last row.

Keystone Species	Features
☐ elephant	• It eats trees and bushes, so grasslands exist where it lives. This allows large herds of animals to have food to eat. • The seeds in its manure often grow into new plants, and the manure acts like fertilizer, so the plants grow well. So the elephant helps with the biodiversity of its ecosystem.
☐ hummingbird	• It flies from flower to flower to feed on nectar. • Around twenty percent of some plants in various regions are pollinated by hummingbirds. Without them, the plant life in certain regions would be much different.
☐ grizzly bear	• It eats large amount of fish, especially salmon. • The leftover fish it does not eat helps make the soil better, so plants grow well and provide food for the animals living in the ecosystem.

B   Read the question again and complete the following paragraph.

One keystone species is _____ . It _____

_____ .

The reason it is a keystone species is that _____

_____

_____ .

Unit 11 Memorable Commercials

Q **What is a slogan from a commercial that you remember? What product was it advertising, and why do you remember it?**

A The following table shows some ideas for answering the question above. Check the one that you like the most. If you have your own idea, write it in the last row.

Slogan	Product
☐ Impossible is nothing.	• The slogan was used in advertisements for Adidas, a company famous for sportswear, especially shoes. • It is an inspiring quote that was made by boxer Muhammad Ali in 1974.
☐ I'm lovin' it.	• This slogan has been used by McDonald's. • The commercials in which the slogan is used make the food look delicious and make the people eating it seem like they are enjoying everything.
☐ Think different.	• This slogan was used in the past by Apple, a computer and electronics manufacturer. • The slogan reminds people that Apple does things differently than others but is still successful.

B Read the question again and complete the following paragraph.

One slogan from a commercial that I remember is _____.

The slogan was used _____

_____.

I remember the slogan because _____

_____.

Unit 12 Marketing through Social Media

Q **What is a social media site people like to use these days? What do people use it for?**

A The following table shows some ideas for answering the question above. Check the one that you like the most. If you have your own idea, write it in the last row.

Social Media Site	Uses
☐ Twitter	• People make posts 140 characters or fewer about any topic that interests them, including their personal lives and sports. • People can retweet comments made by others to indicate that they support those tweets.
☐ Facebook	• People upload pictures and write posts about the various activities that they do in their daily lives. • People set up online stores on Facebook pages and sell goods and services to customers.
☐ Instagram	• People post photographs and videos of themselves doing different activities. • People leave comments about the photographs and videos posted by other individuals.

B Read the question again and complete the following paragraph.

One social media site that people use is _____. People _____
_____.

In addition, _____
_____.

Unit 13 **Medieval Wandering Minstrels**

What type of entertainer would you like to be? What skills are necessary to be that type of entertainer?

A The following table shows some ideas for answering the question above. Check the one that you like the most. If you have your own idea, write it in the last row.

Entertainer	Skills
☐ musician	• A musician is able to play at least one musical instrument and may be able to sing. • A musician must be able to perform in front of a large number of people without getting nervous.
☐ actor/actress	• An actor or actress takes on a role and performs it in a convincing manner in front of an audience. • An actor or actress must memorize dialogue and be able to interact with the other actors and actresses in a performance.
☐ magician	• A magician performs magic tricks that often involve some kind of trickery or special talent. • A magician should be a good performer to make people interested in the tricks that he or she is doing.

B Read the question again and complete the following paragraph.

I would like to be a(n) _____. This type of entertainer _____
_____ .

In addition, _____
_____ .

48

Unit 14 Glass Art

Q Which type of art do you prefer to look at when you visit a gallery or a museum? What are some characteristics of that type of art?

A The following table shows some ideas for answering the question above. Check the one that you like the most. If you have your own idea, write it in the last row.

Art	Characteristics
☐ sculpture	• A sculpture can be made from stone, wood, metal, or even ice. • It typically depicts a person or people, an animal, an object, or an abstract idea.
☐ painting	• A painting is a picture that is made on canvas, paper, or another object by using oil paint or watercolors. • Paintings can show people, landscapes, famous events, objects, and anything else a painter can imagine.
☐ ceramics	• Ceramics are objects that are often made from clay and may be in the shapes of pots, vases, or other containers. • Many ceramics are painted, so they may have designs, people, animals, or other figures on them.

B Read the question again and complete the following paragraph.

When I visit a gallery or a museum, I prefer to look at _____. One characteristic of this type of art is that _____

_____.

Another is that _____

_____.

Unit 15 **Tropical Cyclones**

Q   **What is a violent natural phenomenon? What causes it, and what kind of damage can it do?**

A   The following table shows some ideas for answering the question above. Check the one that you like the most. If you have your own idea, write it in the last row.

Natural Phenomenon	Characteristics
☐ earthquake	• This happens when two or more plates in the Earth's crust move, which results in the ground shaking. • It can cause the ground to split apart and destroy buildings and roads. It can also kill and injure people.
☐ tornado	• This happens when air begins to rotate at very fast speeds, so a funnel is formed. • It can destroy anything that it touches and can travel for long distances before it disappears.
☐ tsunami	• This happens when an earthquake, a volcano, or an explosion causes a large amount of water to be displaced. • A fast-moving wave forms. As it gets closer to shore, the wave becomes larger, so it can cause a great amount of destruction.

B   Read the question again and complete the following paragraph.

One violent natural phenomenon is _____. This happens when _____

_____ .

As a result of it, _____

_____ .

Unit 16 How Ice Ages Occur

Q Do you know of any times in the past when the weather became either very hot or very cold? What were the results of this change in the temperature?

A The following table shows some ideas for answering the question above. Check the one that you like the most. If you have your own idea, write it in the last row.

Hot or Cold Period	Results
☐ Medieval Warm Period	• From around 900 to 1300, increased sunspot activity made global temperatures rise. • Growing seasons were longer, so food was abundant. People grew grapes in England, and the Vikings settled Greenland.
☐ Maunder Minimum	• There was very little sunspot activity on the sun from 1645 to 1715, so temperatures around the world dropped. • Growing seasons became shorter, and glaciers expanded. Winters became long and harsh in many places.
☐ Year without a Summer	• In 1815, the volcano Mount Tambora in Indonesia erupted and sent large amounts of dust into the atmosphere. • The weather was cold all year long in 1816. Crops failed around the world, so people starved in many places.

B Read the question again and complete the following paragraph.

One time when the weather became very hot/cold was _____ .
The reason was that _____
_____ .
As a result, _____
_____ .

MEMO

Fundamental Reading

PLUS